HUNTER HIGH SCHOOL ENTRANCE EXAM

3 PRACTICE HUNTER EXAMS

By

KWELLER PREP

IN COLLABORATION
WITH
ORIGINS TUTORING

Copyright © 2018 Origins Tutoring

All rights reserved. This book or any portion thereof may not be reproduced or used in any manner whatsoever without the express written permission of the publisher.

ISBN: 978-1-948255-55-4

Contents

Part 1. Introduction to the Hunter College High School Admissions Test 1
    Why the Hunter Test? 1
    Who Takes The Hunter Test? 1
    When Does the Hunter Test Take Place? 1
    What's Tested on the Exam? 1
    Length 2
    Format 2
    Multiple Choice 2
    Test Sections 2
    Scoring 3

Part 2. Using This Book 3
    When to Start Studying? 3

Part 3: Exam Preparation and Test-Taking Strategies 4
    Overview 4
    Language Arts Section 4
    Math Section 5
    Essay Section 6
    General Test Taking Strategies to Use on the Hunter Test 7
    Strategies for the Final Days before the Exam 8

Part 4: Managing Test Stress 9
    Handling Test Stress 9
    Preventing and Reducing Test Stress 9

Part 5: Three Practice Tests 11
    Practice Test 1 12
    Test 1 Answer Key and Explanations 33
    Practice Test 2 41
    Test 2 Answer Key and Explanations 62
    Practice Test 3 72
    Test 3 Answer Key and Explanations 93
    Essay Prompts 104

PREPARATION GUIDE

Part 1. Introduction to the Hunter College High School Admissions Test

The Hunter College High School admissions test is an important exam; the more you know about it, the better you will fare. The following section introduces you to the essentials of the Hunter test and all its separate parts.

Why the Hunter Test?

Although children can start at Hunter College Elementary School (HCES) in elementary school, there is only one admission point for the high school: the year of 7th grade. Interested students must do well on the entrance exam to be admitted to the high school.

Who Takes The Hunter Test?

Only students with high scores on their New York state tests can take the Hunter entrance exam. The cut-off score changes every year, but as a rule of thumb only students who score in the 90th percentile will be invited to take the Hunter test. Only children who live in the five boroughs of New York City can attend Hunter, and test-takers need to verify their addresses when applying for the Hunter test.

Not every 5th grade student takes NY state exams, because some schools in New York City have different academic requirements. For students from these schools, they must achieve scores in the 90th percentile for whatever year-end exam is administered by the school. This could be the Iowa test, California Achievement test, State Education Department test, Metropolitan Achievement test, or a similar assessment. Once a student reaches a score in the 90th percentile, both for reading comprehension and math, the child's school can forward these scores directly to the Admissions office at Hunter.

When Does the Hunter Test Take Place?

Prospective students fill out an application in September, then sit for the Hunter test in January of the following year.

What's Tested on the Exam?

The simple answer to the question of what is tested on the Hunter exam is to tell you that it includes sections on math, Language Arts (critical reading) and essay writing.

However, noone except the administrators knows exactly what is on the test, as the format can, and does, vary from year to year. The Hunter test is not like the College Board's SAT or ACT standardized test; you can't easily find practice tests that mimic the exact format and nature of the test in your local bookstore.

So what do we know about the Hunter entrance exam? For starters, we know that the exam is very challenging for 11-year olds, and questions can require students to apply concepts that are taught beyond sixth grade-level curriculum. The test also includes many 'unconventional' questions that require critical rather than linear thinking to solve.

In general, the test requires students to have above-average vocabularies, strong writing and descriptive skills, mental math capabilities, creative problem-solving strategies, critical reading skills, and knowledge of grammar rules. A student's fortitude and time management skills are also tested during the three-hour long exam.

Hunter provides a 'sample' exam on its website for prospective students to download. This, along with the experience of students who have taken the test in previous years, allows some conclusions to be drawn about what students can expect to see on the test. This book offers an overview of the types of questions that are likely to be on the test, some test-taking strategies to improve performance during preparation and on test day, and full-length sample exam/s that students can use to test their knowledge and practice their test-taking skills.

After this overview, look at the breakdowns for each test section to get more information on a specific area of the test.

Length

The Hunter test is a three-hour test. That's nearly as long as the SAT! Because of the length and difficult content of the exam, it is a challenging assignment for sixth-grade students. Individual sections are not timed, so keeping track of time is the test-taker's job.

Format

The entire test is made up of less than 100 questions (the official Hunter *sample* tests have about 35 multiple choice math questions and 47 Critical Reading Questions plus an essay prompt).

**In 2014, HCHS removed Grammar and Usage questions from the sample test. The practice tests in this book also do not include these types of questions. **

Multiple Choice

Apart from the essay, the test is composed of multiple choice questions: a multiple choice math section and multiple choice critical reading/verbal skills section. There is no guessing penalty so students should mark an answer for every question.

Test Sections

ENGLISH LANGUAGE ARTS

During the critical reading subsection, students will see several different reading passages, each followed by approximately five to ten questions. Students should expect to see several different passages. There may be a non-fiction excerpt, several stanzas from a poem, a fictional dialogue, an excerpt from a novel, or a first-person memoir piece.

The possible critical reading questions are just as varied as the passages. There will be questions which ask students to choose what a particular word means in a sentence, as well as questions about the narrator's point of view or the general tone of the passages. Most of the questions ask students to make inferences from the test: these questions give test-takers a phrase from the passage and asks what that phrase suggests about some larger point.

MATH

There are approximately thirty math questions on the official Hunter sample exam, and each question is in multiple choice format.

The questions in the math section cover a wide variety of topics. A few of the questions require students to compute values using decimals, fractions, percents, and whole numbers. In addition to these computation questions, the math problems test students on their ability to apply rules of division, understand probability, calculate rate and averages, use ratios, work with time and money values, find areas and perimeters, and recognize numerical and visual patterns.

Calculator are NOT allowed.

WRITING

The essay section asks students to respond to a specified prompt, and then craft a well-written, proofread writing sample. Originality and strong writing skills can make the difference between being admitted or rejected, so it's key to write an awesome essay during the exam.

Scoring

The scoring process is a little complicated. First, the math and Language Arts sections get scored. Every year, teachers set a cut-off score. Based on these cut-off scores, the top 500 students move to the next round. During the second scoring round, Hunter teachers read the essays. Using the strength of these essays, they choose the top 225-250 students. These students get admissions letters and have the option to join Hunter in 7th grade.

Part 2. Using This Book

You have made an important first step towards ensuring your child will do her best on test day by purchasing this book. "The Hunter Preparation Guide" offers general strategies your child can use to tackle the Hunter test and provides advice on how to prepare and approach specific sections of the test. Your child can also prepare for the exam by taking the practice test/s in this book. Performance on the practice tests can help identify a student's weaknesses and allow your child to focus on concepts that most need to be reviewed. Finally, the seven additional essay prompts will help your child practice writing an essay that impresses and wows the graders.

When to Start Studying?

Every family and student will approach preparation for this test differently. All the children invited to take the Hunter test have scored in the highest percentiles in their age group. There is no 'right' way to prepare; there is only the best way for a particular child and family.

Some students start preparing years in advance before they even know if they will qualify for the test. Others take the 'cram' approach, loading up on as many hours as possible between October and the January test date. Other parents think too much focus on preparation may create anxiety in their child that could backfire on test day. In this case, a more low key approach may work best.

With that said, repeated exposure to the format and nature of the test will help a student prepare for this challenging test. We suggest students, at minimum, take one practice test (preferably under timed conditions) and spend a minimum of 8-10 hours of practicing reading comprehension questions, studying vocab, and working through challenging math problems. Trying a few sample essays within a time limit is also important.

As they say, knowledge is power! And preparing for the Hunter test also gives students a chance to know what they are up against. This alone can help a sixth-grader not panic on test day when faced with unfamiliar and perplexing questions. The Hunter test measures a student's academic performance but also his or her ability to manage time efficiently and capacity to keep his or her wits under pressure.

Part 3: Exam Preparation and Test-Taking Strategies

Preparing for the Hunter test in many ways follows the same process as preparing for any other exam—your child needs to review the concepts he or she already knows and boost skills in areas that he or she is unfamiliar with. You can diagnose your child's weaknesses by analyzing her scores on the practice tests in this book. Then, focus study time on reviewing and practicing more of the question types that the student finds tricky or regularly stumbles on. There are also a number of general test-taking strategies and tips that specifically apply to standardized tests that will help your child perform at her best on exam day.

Overview

For the Language Arts section, students should try to build up their vocabularies through reading lots of different texts. This will also help students get more comfortable with critical reading questions and understanding the main arguments in a passage. On the other side, strong quantitative reasoning skills are essential on test day, and students can prepare by doing advanced math, including tackling unconventional math problems. Finally, the essay is the deciding factor for admission. Students should practice responding to prompts and sharing plenty of descriptive details. Engaging the grader is essential for achieving a top score.

Language Arts Section

CRITICAL READING

The format of the reading comprehension section should be fairly familiar to students, but the passages will be a little more advanced than what students are used to in the 5th and 6th grade curriculum.

Since test-takers can complete the exam in any order, students can work on each section at their own pace, which can be a benefit on long critical reading passages. Students can work on one passage at a time, or skip to later passages and then return to the beginning of the critical reading questions, or choose any other order that feels helpful.

The test will have passages from a variety of genres. There will be fiction and non-fiction excerpts, stanzas from a poem, a dialogue, or a memoir piece. A good way to get ready for these questions is reading a variety of texts and building up reading skills naturally.

In addition to reading experience, students should develop a strategy for understanding words in context. For example, when your child reads a passage, suggest that she circle any new words that she doesn't understand. Then, ask her to look in the context to find clues--words or phrases that hint at what the new word means. Next, using these clues ask her to ask herself, "What word do I know that would make sense in the place of the new word in this sentence?" Then she can substitute the familiar word in the sentence and read the passage to see if the word makes sense in the passage. These skills will come in handy for the entire Language Arts section.

Preparation Guide

Tips for the Critical Reading Section

- **Pace Yourself**
Do not spend too much time on any one item. Skip an item if necessary, leave it blank, and come back to it later. Focus on the questions that come quicker and easier for you.

- **Skim When Needed**
Skimming can be an important strategy at times. For example, if you are asked to choose a definition for a word in the passage, the word will usually be italicized. Scan the passage to find the word. Reading the sentence before the sentence containing the word, and the sentence following the word will usually give you enough information to answer the question correctly. Or if the question asks about the setting of a story, skim the paragraphs until you find the ones that discuss the time and the place, which together would make up the setting. Now, read this part of the passage carefully.

- **Always Refer Back to the Passage**
When answering the questions, refer back to the passage. Choose the answer that is given in the passage, even if there is another answer that you know is factually correct.

Math Section

On the Hunter entrance exam, test-takers have to answer approximately thirty multiple-choice math questions. The questions cover a variety of topics, including:

- Computing values using decimals, fractions, percentages, and whole numbers
- Probability
- Rules of division/multiplication and basic operations
- Rates and averages
- Ratios
- Time and money
- Areas, perimeters, and geometry
- Numerical and visual patterns

Some topics on the math section are straightforward, such as the computation questions or basic geometry problems. As long as test-takers have done well in math at school, they should not have a problem on these questions.

In addition to these questions, the Hunter test is known for word problems and tricky possible answer choices. Because no calculators are allowed, students need to build up their mental math skills and make sure they're able to do paper and pencil calculations during the exam. Some of the questions bring several topics into play at once, so test-takers should do plenty of sample word problems with multi-step solutions.

The math section generally starts with easier questions and moves toward more difficult questions, so students should keep this progression in mind. Because the sections are not timed individually, students need to keep track of how long each question takes and pace themselves. In general, the best way to prepare for the math section is through lots of practice. Students need to develop a reliable strategy for approaching tough problems, such as building a model, drawing a picture, using have/need boxes, or estimating possible answers. By practicing these techniques, it'll be easier for students to jump into tough problems on the exam.

Tips for the Math Section

- **Get Rid of Answer Choices.**
  Sometimes tough math problems seem confusing, but students can take steps to eliminate choices that are obviously wrong. Figuring out that the answer must be positive (or negative) or greater than a certain number will get rid of some options.

- **Find an Answer Before Reading the Choices.**
  Sometimes it's easy to look at the answers before solving a problem. For math questions, that's not the correct strategy. Students should try solving the problem first before checking the possible answers.

- **Think Creatively.**
  There are plenty of math problems on the exam that could be solved either by tedious, lengthy calculations or a clever strategy; noticing these shortcuts and thinking creatively helps students shave off minutes and use that time in better ways.

Essay Section

The Hunter website provides general guidelines for the writing assignment, asking students to write either an essay or an autobiographical piece that "demonstrate the originality, effectiveness, and use of detail in your writing."

Thus, the essay section is the opportunity for students to show writing mastery. The goal is to impress the reader with their descriptive abilities, skills with figurative language, and storytelling capabilities.

In previous years, the writing assignment asked students to tell a story, write about something they experienced, and use sensory details that somehow relate to New York City. Only children who live in the five boroughs can attend Hunter, so with this prompt every person taking the test will have something unique to share about the city.

However, the prompt changes each year on the essay section, and so students need to be prepared to face a variety of topics. For example, in 2016, students were asked to choose between two essay choices and neither of the options was NYC-focused.

There is no required length for the essay, but writing the equivalent of about five paragraphs is a reasonable goal (the exam booklet provides two pages). A quick brainstorming session will help students think of key memories, places, and important details to share, and a short outline with those ideas can help students stay on track. Students will be provided with paper in the test booklet to brainstorm ideas and write a draft before writing the final essay. Because the exam does not have timed sections, each student should have a clear idea of how long it takes him or her to produce a proof-read essay.

Since a top essay score is essential for admission, students should aim to write essays that are unique, engaging, and show off strong writing abilities. Engaged graders are the goal! With this in mind, test-takers should think of a list of familiar places and strong memories that they can describe with plenty of detail. On test day, this list will come in handy.

> ## Tips for the Essay Section
>
> - **Make a plan.**
>   Jot down an outline or some notes on how you will structure and approach your answer to the question given.
> - **Choose subjects you are comfortable with.**
>   Don't necessarily structure your essay on the truest answer or the one you think will impress readers. Instead, choose something you can write well about. A well-articulated, emotionally poignant example is better than one that has impressive content but is poorly written.
> - **Aim to have an emotional impact on the reader.**
>   Include a lot of references to sensory perceptions and emotions. Use vivid details and imagery to get your points and examples across.

General Test Taking Strategies to Use on the Hunter Test

If your child knows the material on which she will be tested, it will improve her chances of succeeding. But it does not guarantee that she will do her best on the exam. The Hunter test does not just test your child's knowledge of and skills in English, math, and writing. Like all standardized tests, it also measures her test-taking skills. We recommend you introduce and/or remind your child of general test-taking strategies that could help her perform her very best on test day. Please keep in mind that the strategies mentioned here are not hard and fast rules. They are flexible. If your child feels they don't work for him, then alter them to suit his needs.

- **Mark up the test.**
  Mark up the booklet as much as you need to as you take the test. If you find something that looks important, underline it, make notes in the margins, circle facts, cross out answers you know are wrong, and draw diagrams.

- **Answer questions on the test booklet.**
  Circle the answers for all the questions in one section of the test before you transfer them to the answer sheet (for the English and reading tests,, transfer your answers after each passage, and for the math transfer them at the end of each page). This serves two purposes: First, it allows you to concentrate on choosing the right answer and not filling in bubbles. Second, it keeps you from skipping an answer and mis-numbering your entire test if you decide to return to a difficult question later.

- **Never leave an answer blank.**
  The Hunter test does not deduct points for wrong answers. This means there is no penalty for guessing. With this in mind, you should answer every question, even if it is a total guess. If you do find a question that completely stumps you, look through the answers and try to find at least one that you know is wrong. The more answers you eliminate, the better the odds that your guess will be the correct answer.

- **Answer easy questions first.**
  Students can answer questions in whatever order they prefer, and there's no guessing penalty. That means students should aim for easy questions first to score points, and then they should try hard questions at the end.

- **Read each question carefully.**
  Some students race through test questions without taking in all the information. There are lots of trick answers that seem correct on the Hunter test, which means students have to read carefully and think

before jumping to a particular answer. It is easy when pressed for time to misread a question and get the answer wrong. Missing a word like "except" can lead you to answer the question incorrectly.

- **Read all the answers.**

    If one answer jumps out at you and you are sure it is right, read all the other answers anyway. Something may seem right just because the Hunter test writers have put it there to make you think it might be the right answer. Spend the time to go through all the answers, at least quickly.

- **Pace yourself.**

    The exam is given within a three hour time limit, but it's up to students to pace themselves. Students should make sure to bring a watch and track how long they spend on questions. If you find one question is taking too long, circle it in the test book and return to it later.

- **Ignore all distractions.**

    You may have tried to re-create the exact test-taking atmosphere during your practice exams. But when you go for the real thing you will be in a room with many other people, maybe even someone with a cold who is sneezing or coughing. Ignore it all and concentrate on your test.

- **Relax.**

    Take a deep breath. Put everything in perspective. Give yourself a pep talk: You are prepared and know what to expect.

Strategies for the Final Days before the Exam

Your weeks or months of preparation will soon pay off. You have worked hard, and the test is just a week away. Here are some tips for making sure things go smoothly in the home stretch.

The Week before the Test:

- Be sure you know exactly where you are taking the test. Get detailed directions. Take a practice transit trip so you know exactly how long it will take to get there.
- Review everything you have learned.
- Get quality sleep each night.
- Practice visualization - see yourself performing well on the Hunter test.

The Day before the Test:

- Get to bed early.
- Get light exercise.
- Get everything you will need ready: pencils/pens, a watch, admission materials/documentation, and water or any mints or snacks you would like to have along.
- Make a list of everything you need to bring so you don't forget anything in the morning.

The Day of the Test:

- Eat a light, healthy breakfast, such as yogurt and granola or a low-fat, low-sugar cereal and fruit.
- Dress comfortably. Wear layers so that you can take off a sweatshirt or sweater if you are too warm in the test room.

At the Test Site:

- Avoid squeezing in a last-minute review. Instead, visualize your success and plan your reward for after the test is over.
- Think positive. When there's a frustrating question, don't freeze up and start thinking all kinds of negative ideas,

What to Bring to the Test

- ✓ Picture ID
- ✓ Admission slip
- ✓ A watch
- ✓ Water
- ✓ Two number 2 pencils with erasers and two black or blue ink pens
- ✓ Sweatshirt or sweater

which kills self-esteem during the exam. Instead, use positive self-talk, including "I've studied this," "I can do this," and "I can figure this problem out."
- If you find yourself getting anxious, remember to calm yourself by taking long, deep breaths.

Part 4: Managing Test Stress

Handling Test Stress

Test anxiety is like the common cold. Most people suffer from it periodically. It won't kill you, but it can make your life miserable for several days.

Like a cold, test anxiety can be mild or severe. A student may just feel an underlying nervousness about the upcoming exam. Or she may be nearly paralyzed with worry, especially if there is a lot riding on the exam. Whatever the case, if your child has test anxiety, you can help her cope with it. Fortunately, many strategies help prevent and treat test anxiety.

Preventing and Reducing Test Stress

The best cure for test anxiety is to prevent it from happening in the first place. Test anxiety is often caused by a lack of preparation. If you learn all you can about the test and create and follow a study plan, your child should be in good shape when it comes to exam time. Here are some other, more general strategies:

- Establish and stick to routine. Routines help us feel more comfortable and in control. Whenever possible, have your child study at the same time and in the same place. Make test preparation a habit that is hard to break.
- Keep general stress level low. Remember to encourage your child to keep things in perspective. Tell her not to worry about things beyond her control. Instead, suggest that she thinks of how she can handle what is in her control (like a solid study routine!).

If your child still feels a lot of stress despite a study plan and test preparation, here are some additional strategies to help reduce stress:

☐ **Face fears.** Help your child realize that fears are useless and only paralyze and keep him from studying and doing well on the exam. Acknowledge his fears, but help him put them in perspective.

One helpful strategy is to ask your child to write down his fears. Putting worries on paper makes them seem more manageable than when they are bouncing around in his brain and keeping him up at night. Once his fears are written down, he can then brainstorm solutions. That will help him feel more in control.

☐ **Keep things in perspective.** Yes, the Hunter test is an important test, but it needs to be put in context. Tell your child that even if he does poorly on the exam, it is not the end of the world. His family won't stop loving him. He won't be less of a person. Perspective is important to performance. Of course your child should be serious about succeeding. But he should not lose sight of other important aspects of life.

☐ **Be sufficiently prepared.** Have your child create a study plan based on the number of weeks or months she has decided to devote to preparation for the test. Anxiety often comes from feeling insecure in a new situation. But if your child prepares well, using this book, the Hunter test will not be entirely new to him. He will know how to answer the questions.

☐ **Tell your child imagine herself succeeding.** Highly successful people will often tell you that one of their secrets is visualization. In their mind's eye, they see themselves succeeding. They imagine the situations they will face, and then imagine themselves handling those situations beautifully.

Visualization is a powerful tool. If your child believes she can accomplish something, she is far more likely to accomplish it. Likewise, if she believe she can't do something, she is far more likely to fail to achieve that goal.

Positive visualization will make it easier for your child to study and manage the test preparation process. Anyone can use the power of visualization. Your child can try the following visualization: "Picture yourself sitting calmly through the exam, answering one question after another correctly. See yourself getting excellent test results in the mail. Picture yourself receiving the Hunter acceptance letter you desire.

It is difficult for a child to do her best on a test when she is not feeling well. Her mind and body need to be in good shape for the test. Here are some specific suggestions for staying healthy throughout the entire test-preparation process and especially in the week before the exam:

❑ **Get enough rest.** A good night's rest before the exam will make sure your child is able to concentrate the day of the exam. If she has trouble sleeping, encourage her to try one of the following strategies:

- Get exercise during the day. A tired body will demand more sleep.

- Relax with a hot bath, a good book, or sleep-inducing foods. A glass of warm milk, for example, may help her fall back asleep.

- Do some gentle stretching or seated forward bends. Or, practice a few relaxation poses from yoga.

- Spend a few minutes doing deep breathing. Fill your lungs slowly and completely. Hold for a few seconds and then release slowly and completely. You can practice deep breathing any time you need to relax or regain focus.

- Write down your worries. Again, putting your fears on paper can help make them more manageable.

❑ **Eat well.** How your child eats has a big impact of how she performs on test day. Her body needs nutrition to perform at its best. Foods to especially avoid at test time include high-sugar, high calorie, low-nutrition foods, such as doughnuts, chips, and cookies. Instead, find healthy substitutes.

Practice Test 1

Student's Name: _____	Admissions ID Code: _____
Student's Signature: _____	Date of Birth: _____

PRACTICE TEST 1 FOR HUNTER COLLEGE HIGH SCHOOL EXAMINATION

(THIS TEST WAS CREATED BASED ON A SAMPLE TEST PROVIDED BY HUNTER COLLEGE HIGH SCHOOL)

This test contains three sections: 46 multiple-choice **English Language Arts questions**, **a Writing Assignment**, and 35 multiple-choice **Mathematics questions**.

Each multiple-choice question is followed by **five possible answers: A, B, C, D, or E.** Choose the best answer for each question. You may make marks in this test booklet; use the space between questions and the blank pages in your booklet for scrap paper. **There is no penalty for guessing.**

On the answer sheet, carefully blacken the circle that contains the letter of the answer you select. Use only a Number 2 pencil for the multiple-choice sections. If you wish to change an answer, carefully erase the wrong answer completely and mark your new answer. **As soon as you finish one section of the test, go on to the next section. Monitor the time the proctor writes on the board.**

Calculators are not permitted.

You have a total of **three hours to complete the examination**, including the Writing Assignment.

If you complete the test before the time is up, review your previous work to correct for errors. Make sure that your answer sheet is accurately and cleanly prepared.

You may not remove any page from this booklet or take papers from the test room.

Kweller Prep

LANGUAGE ARTS
Critical Reading

Each of the following passages is followed by questions based on its content. Choose the letter of the answer that best reflects what is stated or implied by the passage.

Reading Passage A
adapted from the short story "The Sound of Summer Running"
by Ray Bradbury

1   Late that night, going home from the show with his mother and father and his brother Tom, Douglas saw the tennis shoes in the bright store window. He glanced quickly away, but his ankles were seized, his feet suspended, then rushed. The earth spun; the shop awnings slammed their canvas wings overhead with the thrust of his
5   body running. His mother and father and brother walked quietly on both sides of him. Douglas walked backward, watching the tennis shoes in the midnight window left behind.

"It was a nice movie," said Mother.

Douglas murmured, "It was. . . ."

10 It was June and long past time for buying the special shoes that were quiet as a summer rain falling on the walks. June and the earth full of raw power and everything everywhere in motion. The grass was still pouring in from the country, surrounding the sidewalks, stranding the houses. Any moment the town would capsize, go down and leave not a stir in the clover and weeds. And here Douglas
15 stood, trapped on the dead cement and the red-brick streets, hardly able to move.

"Dad!" He blurted it out. "Back there in that window, those Cream-Sponge Para Litefoot Shoes . . ."

His father didn't even turn. "Suppose you tell me why you need a new pair of sneakers. Can you do that?"

20 "Well . . ."

It was because they felt the way it feels every summer when you take off your shoes for the first time and run in the grass. They felt like it feels sticking your feet out of the hot covers in wintertime to let the cold wind from the open window blow on them suddenly and you let them stay out a long time until you pull them back in under the covers again to feel them, like packed snow. The tennis shoes felt
25 like it always feels the first time every year wading in the slow waters of the creek and seeing your feet below, half an inch further downstream, with refraction, than the real part of you above water.

"Dad," said Douglas, "it's hard to explain."

Somehow the people who made tennis shoes knew what boys needed and wanted. They put marshmallows and coiled springs in the soles and they wove the
30 rest out of grasses bleached and fired in the wilderness. Somewhere deep in the soft loam of the shoes the thin hard sinews of the buck deer were hidden. The people that made the shoes must have watched a lot of winds blow the trees and a lot of rivers going down to the lakes. Whatever it was, it was in the shoes, and it was summer. Douglas tried to get all this in words.

35 "Yes," said Father, "but what's wrong with last year's sneakers? Why can't you dig them out of the closet?"

Well, he felt sorry for boys who lived in California where they wore tennis shoes all year and never knew what it was to get winter off your feet, peel off the iron leather shoes all full of snow and rain and run barefoot for a day and then
40   lace on the first new tennis shoes of the season, which was better than barefoot. The magic was always in the new pair of shoes. The magic might die by the first of September, but now in late June there was still plenty of magic, and shoes like these could jump you over trees and rivers and houses. And if you wanted, they could jump you over fences and sidewalks and dogs.
45   "Don't you see?" said Douglas. "I just can't use last year's pair."
     For last year's pair were dead inside. They had been fine when he started them out, last year. But by the end of summer, every year, you always found out, you always knew, you couldn't really jump over rivers and trees and houses in them, and they were dead. But this was a new year, and he felt that this time, with this new
50   pair of shoes, he could do anything, anything at all.

1. In this selection, the narrator associates new shoes with
   (A) winter
   (B) misunderstanding
   (C) freedom
   (D) misery
   (E) childhood

2. In line 39, Douglas mentions the sensation of taking off "iron shoes." He describes his winter shoes this way in order to suggest they are
   (A) valuable
   (B) insignificant
   (C) heavy and confining
   (D) the color of metal
   (E) ordinary and boring

3. In the first paragraph, when Douglas first spots the shoes in the window, his reaction might be described as
   (A) bored
   (B) mildly interested
   (C) transfixed
   (D) amused
   (E) helpless

4. When Douglas' mother mentions the movie in line 9, his reaction to her shows he is
   (A) interested
   (B) overjoyed
   (C) annoyed
   (D) distracted
   (E) depressed

5. In this passage, Douglas' father
   (A) is worried about spending money on other things.
   (B) wants to buy his son a pair of shoes.
   (C) ignores his son.
   (D) doesn't understand the "magic" of a new pair of shoes.
   (E) feels sorry for his son.

6. The refraction the narrator describes in line 26 causes
   (A) a visual distortion
   (B) a chilling sensation
   (C) a buzzing in the ears
   (D) a warm feeling
   (E) physical harm

7. In line 37, Douglas feels sorry for boys in California because they
   (A) Never get to experience snow
   (B) Have to deal with horrible weather
   (C) Never get to experience the thrill of having new sneakers
   (D) Have to wear uncomfortable shoes
   (E) Don't get to run and play outside very often

8. In this passage, Douglas might best be described as
   (A) imaginative
   (B) indifferent
   (C) manipulative
   (D) deceptive
   (E) genius

Critical Reading Passage B
adapted from the short story "The Monkey's Paw"
by W. W. Jacobs

1   "What was that you started telling me the other day about a monkey's paw or something, Morris?" asked Mr. White.

"Nothing," said the soldier, <u>hastily</u>. "Leastways nothing worth hearing."

"Monkey's paw?" said Mrs. White, curiously.

5   "Well, it's just a bit of what you might call magic, perhaps," said the sergeant-major, offhandedly.

His three listeners leaned forward eagerly. The visitor absent-mindedly put his empty glass to his lips and then set it down again. His host filled it for him.

"To look at," said the sergeant-major, fumbling in his pocket, "it's just an
10   ordinary little paw, dried to a mummy."

He took something out of his pocket and proffered it. Mrs. White drew back with a grimace, but her son, taking it, examined it curiously.

"And what is there special about it?" inquired Mr. White as he took it from his son, and having examined it, placed it upon the table.

15   "It had a spell put on it by an old man," said the sergeant-major, "a very holy man. He wanted to show that fate ruled people's lives, and that those who interfered with it did so to their sorrow. He put a spell on it so that three separate men could each have three wishes from it."

His manner was so impressive that his hearers were conscious that their light
20   laughter jarred somewhat.

"Well, why don't you have three, sir?" said Herbert White, cleverly.

The soldier regarded him in the way that middle age is wont to regard <u>presumptuous</u> youth. "I have," he said, quietly, and his blotchy face whitened.

"And did you really have the three wishes granted?" asked Mrs. White.

25   "I did," said the sergeant-major, and his glass tapped against his strong teeth.

"And has anybody else wished?" persisted the old lady.

"The first man had his three wishes. Yes," was the reply; "I don't know what the first two were, but the third was for death. That's how I got the paw."

His tones were so grave that a hush fell upon the group.

30   "If you've had your three wishes, it's no good to you now, then, Morris," said the old man at last. "What do you keep it for?"

The soldier shook his head. "<u>Fancy</u>, I suppose," he said, slowly. "I did have some idea of selling it, but I don't think I will. It has caused enough mischief already.
35   Besides, people won't buy. They think it's a fairy tale; some of them, and those who do think anything of it want to try it first and pay me afterward."

"If you could have another three wishes," said the old man, eyeing him keenly, "would you have them?"

"I don't know," said the other. "I don't know."

He took the paw, and dangling it between his forefinger and thumb, suddenly
40   threw it upon the fire. White, with a slight cry, stooped down and snatched it off.

"Better let it burn," said the soldier, solemnly.

"If you don't want it, Morris," said the other, "give it to me."

"I won't," said his friend, doggedly. "I threw it on the fire. If you keep it, don't blame me for what happens. Pitch it on the fire again like a sensible man."

45 The other shook his head and examined his new possession closely. "How do you do it?" he inquired.

"Hold it up in your right hand and wish aloud," said the sergeant-major, "but I warn you of the consequences."

9. As used in line 3, "hastily" means
   (A) desperately
   (B) hurriedly
   (C) easily
   (D) slowly
   (E) carelessly

10. The mood of the passage is one of
    (A) hopelessness
    (B) humor
    (C) distaste
    (D) hope
    (E) suspense

11. As used in line 23, the best synonym for "presumptuous" is
    (A) friendly
    (B) optimistic
    (C) arrogant
    (D) submissive
    (E) ignorant

12. The sergeant-major's attitude toward the paw is
    (A) wary
    (B) vengeful
    (C) indifferent
    (D) terrified
    (E) welcoming

13. When the sergeant-major first begins discussing the paw in line 5, the Whites' reaction shows they are
    (A) enraptured by his story about the paw
    (B) not interested in what he has to say
    (C) afraid of him and his past
    (D) bored by his words
    (E) interested in something else

14. Mr. White's attitude toward the paw is one of
    (A) rage
    (B) envy
    (C) curiosity
    (D) desperation
    (E) distress

15. In line the context of line 32, "fancy" means
    (A) unknowingly
    (B) for mysterious reasons
    (C) for the sake of memory
    (D) on a whim
    (E) highly decorative

Critical Reading Passage C
adapted from the short story "A White Heron"
By Sarah Orne Jewitt

1   Sylvia is horror-stricken to hear a clear whistle not very far away. Not a bird's-whistle, which would have a sort of friendliness, but a boy's whistle, determined, and somewhat aggressive. Sylvia left her cow to whatever sad fate might await her, and stepped discreetly aside into the bushes, but she was just too late.

5   The enemy had discovered her, and called out in a very cheerful and persuasive tone, "Halloa, little girl, how far is it to the road?" and trembling Sylvia answered almost <u>inaudibly</u>, "A good ways."

     She did not dare to look boldly at the tall young man, who carried a gun over his shoulder, but she came out of her bush and again followed the cow, while he

10   walked alongside.

     "I have been hunting for some birds," the stranger said kindly, "and I have lost my way, and need a friend very much. Don't be afraid," he added <u>gallantly</u>. "Speak up and tell me what your name is, and whether you think I can spend the night at your house, and go out gunning early in the morning."

15   Sylvia was more alarmed than before. Would not her grandmother consider her much to blame? But who could have foreseen such an accident as this? It did not seem to be her fault, and she hung her head as if the stem of it were broken, but managed to answer "Sylvy," with much effort when her companion again asked her name.

20   Mrs. Tilley was standing in the doorway when the trio came into view. The cow gave a loud moo by way of explanation.

     "Yes, you'd better speak up for yourself, <u>you old trial</u>! Where'd she tucked herself away this time, Sylvy?" But Sylvia kept an awed silence; she knew by instinct that her grandmother did not comprehend the gravity of the situation. She

25   must be mistaking the stranger for one of the farmer-lads of the region.

     The young man stood his gun beside the door, and dropped a lumpy game-bag beside it; then he bade Mrs. Tilley good-evening, and repeated his wayfarer's story, and asked if he could have a night's lodging.

     "Put me anywhere you like," he said. "I must be off early in the morning,

30   before day; but I am very hungry, indeed. You can give me some milk at any rate, that's plain."

     "Dear sakes, yes," responded the hostess, whose long slumbering hospitality seemed to be easily awakened. "You might fare better if you went out to the main road a mile or so, but you 're welcome to what we 've got. I'll milk right off, and

35   you make yourself at home. You can sleep on husks or feathers," she proffered graciously. "I raised them all myself. There 's good pasturing for geese just below here towards the ma'sh. Now step round and set a plate for the gentleman, Sylvy!"

Critical Reading

16. In line 1, when Sylvia first encounters she young man, she feels
    (A) excited
    (B) afraid
    (C) conflicted
    (D) curious
    (E) angry

17. In line 7, "inaudibly" means
    (A) loudly
    (B) unable to be heard
    (C) excitedly
    (D) shyly
    (E) boldly

18. In line 12, "gallantly" means
    (A) with no regard another's feelings
    (B) like a gentleman
    (C) spitefully
    (D) mysteriously
    (E) perfectly

19. In line 22, when Mrs. Tilley refers to "you old trial," she is speaking to
    (A) her pet dog
    (B) the young man
    (C) Sylvia
    (D) herself
    (E) the cow

20. The young man needs Syvlia's help because he
    (A) wants to meet her grandmother
    (B) has lost one of his own cows
    (C) has lost his way
    (D) is hurt
    (E) needs a hunting companion

21. Based on her interactions with the young man, Mrs. Tilley might be described as
    (A) grumpy
    (B) suspicious
    (C) afraid
    (D) welcoming
    (E) tired

Critical Reading Passage D
adapted from the short story "The Masque of the Red Death"
By Edgar Allan Poe

1   The seventh apartment was closely shrouded in black velvet tapestries that hung all over the ceiling and down the walls, falling in heavy folds upon a carpet of the same material and hue. But in this chamber only, the color of the windows failed to correspond with the decorations. The panes here were scarlet—a deep blood color.
5   Now in no one of the seven apartments was there any lamp or candelabrum, amid the profusion of golden ornaments that lay scattered to and fro or depended from the roof. There was no light of any kind emanating from lamp or candle within the suite of chambers. But in the corridors that followed the suite, there stood, opposite to each window, a heavy tripod, bearing a brazier of fire that projected its rays
10   through the tinted glass and so glaringly illumined the room. And thus were produced a multitude of gaudy and fantastic appearances. But in the western or black chamber the effect of the fire-light that streamed upon the dark hangings through the blood-tinted panes, was ghastly in the extreme, and produced so wild a look upon the countenances of those who entered, that there were few of the company
15   bold enough to set foot within its precincts at all.

       It was in this apartment, also, that there stood against the western wall, a gigantic clock of ebony. Its pendulum swung to and fro with a dull, heavy, monotonous clang; and when the minute-hand made the circuit of the face, and the hour was to be stricken, there came from the brazen lungs of the clock a sound which was clear
20   and loud and deep and exceedingly musical, but of so peculiar a note and emphasis that, at each lapse of an hour, the musicians of the orchestra were constrained to pause, momentarily, in their performance, to hearken to the sound; and thus the waltzers perforce ceased their evolutions; and there was a brief disconcert of the whole gay company; and, while the chimes of the clock yet rang, it was observed
25   that the giddiest grew pale, and the more aged and sedate passed their hands over their brows as if in confused reverie or meditation. But when the echoes had fully ceased, a light laughter at once pervaded the assembly; the musicians looked at each other and smiled as if at their own nervousness and folly, and made whispering vows, each to the other, that the next chiming of the clock should produce in them
30   no similar emotion; and then, after the lapse of sixty minutes, (which embrace three thousand and six hundred seconds of the Time that flies,) there came yet another chiming of the clock, and then were the same disconcert and tremulousness and meditation as before.

Critical Reading

22. In line 1, shrouded means
    (A) bared
    (B) hidden
    (C) decorated
    (D) enlivened
    (E) wrapped

23. In line 6, "profusion" means
    (A) lack of
    (B) wide variety
    (C) a large quantity
    (D) a small number
    (E) absence

24. Based on the context provide, the "brazier" mentioned in line 10 is
    (A) something dangerous
    (B) an elaborate decoration
    (C) a heavy tripod
    (D) a container that holds coals or fire
    (E) an ebony clock

25. The apartment, or room, described in the first paragraph could best be characterized as
    (A) busy
    (B) plain
    (C) exciting
    (D) pleasant
    (E) frightening

26. The world "countenances" as it appears in line 14 means
    (A) body language
    (B) clothing
    (C) bodies
    (D) masks
    (E) faces

27. What happens each time the clock, described in the second paragraph, chimes the hour?
    (A) people laugh and ignore it
    (B) everything else happening at the party stops
    (C) the musicians play louder
    (D) the dancers waltz even faster
    (E) the red and black room glows

28. In line 30, the musicians vow that
    (A) the party will be a success no matter what
    (B) they will investigate the clock
    (C) they will play beautiful music
    (D) they will escape the party whenever they can
    (E) the next hour the clock won't catch them off guard

Kweller Prep

Critical Reading Passage E
adapted from the poem *The Rime of the Ancient Mariner*
By Samuel Taylor Coleridge

1   The ship was cheered, the harbour cleared,
       Merrily did we drop
       Below the kirk, below the hill,
       Below the light-house top.

5   The Sun came up upon the left,
       Out of the sea came he!
       And he shone bright, and on the right
       Went down into the sea

       And now the STORM-BLAST came, and he
10   Was tyrannous and strong:
       He struck with his o'ertaking wings,
       And chased south along.

       With sloping masts and dipping prow,
       As who pursued with yell and blow
15   Still treads the shadow of his foe
       And forward bends his head,
       The ship drove fast, loud roared the blast,
       And southward aye we fled.

       And now there came both mist and snow,
20   And it grew wondrous cold;
       And ice, mast-high, came floating by,
       As green as emerald.

       And through the drifts the snowy clifts
       Did send a <u>dismal</u> sheen:
25   Nor shapes of men nor beasts we ken—
       The ice was all between.

       The ice was here, the ice was here, the ice was there,
       The ice was all around:
       It crack and growled, and roared and howled.
30   Like noises in a swound!

Critical Reading

29. In the first two stanzas, the mood is
    (A) serious
    (B) foreboding
    (C) silly
    (D) cheerful
    (E) apathetic

30. In line 9, the "he" mentioned is
    (A) the storm
    (B) one of the sailors
    (C) the sun
    (D) the captain of the ship
    (E) the ice

31. The speaker says, in line 29 that the ice "cracked and growled, and roared and howled." This shows the ice to be
    (A) annoying
    (B) friendly
    (C) threatening
    (D) a hindrance
    (E) unconcerned

32. The storm in the third stanza is described as
    (A) cheerful
    (B) powerful
    (C) harmless
    (D) unavoidable
    (E) kind

33. In line 24, dismal means
    (A) fortunate
    (B) dangerous
    (C) gloomy
    (D) bright
    (E) intriguing

Critical Reading Passage F
adapted from the Essay, "When Chocolate was Medicine"
By Christina A. Jones

1   In the seventeenth century, Europeans who had not traveled overseas tasted coffee, hot chocolate, and tea for the very first time. For this brand new clientele, the brews of foreign beans and leaves carried within them the wonder and danger of far-away lands. They were classified at first not as food, but as drugs — pleasant-tasting,
5   with recommended dosages prescribed by pharmacists and physicians, and dangerous when self-administered. As they warmed to the use and abuse of hot beverages, Europeans frequently experienced moral and physical confusion brought on by frothy pungency, unpredictable effects, and even (rumor had it) fatality. Madame de Sévigné, marquise and diarist of court life, famously cautioned her daughter about chocolate
10   in a letter when its effects still inspired awe tinged with fear: "And what do we make of chocolate? Are you not afraid that it will burn your blood? Could it be that these miraculous effects mask some kind of inferno [in the body]?"

        These mischievously potent drugs were met with widespread curiosity and concern. In response, a written tradition of treatises was born over the course of
15   the seventeenth and eighteenth centuries. Physicians and tradesmen who claimed knowledge of fields from pharmacology to etiquette proclaimed the many health benefits of hot drinks or issued <u>impassioned</u> warnings about their abuse. The resulting textual tradition documents how the tonics were depicted during the first century of their hotly debated place among Europe's delicacies.

20   Chocolate was the first of the three to enter the pharmaceutical annals in Europe via a medical essay published in Madrid in 1631: *Curioso Tratado de la naturaleza y calidad del chocolate* by Antonio Colmenero de Ledesma. Colmenero's short treatise dates from the era when Spain was the main importer of chocolate. Spain had occupied the Aztec territories since the time of Cortés in
25   the 1540s — the first Spanish-language description of chocolate dates from the 1552 — whereas the British and French were only beginning to establish a colonial presence in the Caribbean and South America during the 1620s and 30s. Having acquired a degree in medicine and served a Jesuit mission in the colonies, Colmenero was as close as one could come to a European expert on the pharma-
30   ceutical qualities of the cacao bean. Classified as medical literature in libraries today, Colmenero's work introduced chocolate to Europe as a drug by appealing to the science of the humors, or essential bodily fluids.

        "Humoralism," a theory of health and illness inherited from Hippocrates and Galen was still influential in 1630. It held that the body was composed of four
35   essential liquids: black bile, blood, yellow bile, and phlegm. Each humor echoed one of the four elements of nature—earth, air, fire, and water—and exhibited particular properties that changed the body's disposition: black bile was cold and dry, blood was hot and wet, yellow bile felt hot and dry, and phlegm made the body cold and wet. Balanced together, they maintained the healthy functioning of an organism.
40   When the balance among them tipped and one occurred in excess, it produced symptoms of what we now call "disease" in the body. While common European pharmaceuticals had long been classified as essentially cooling or heating, cacao presented both hot and cold characteristics. Later treatises faced the same <u>conundrum</u> regarding coffee. Depending on how it was administered/ingested, hot chocolate's
45   curative effects also crisscrossed the humoral categories in unexpected ways.

Critical Reading

34. In the seventeenth century, Europeans believe chocolate was
    (A) a delicious, exotic food
    (B) a dangerous drug
    (C) a form of currency
    (D) one of the humors
    (E) a toy for children

35. In line 17, "impassioned" means
    (A) intelligent
    (B) cautionary
    (C) unfeeling
    (D) with strong feelings
    (E) logical

36. "Humoralism," as mentioned in this passage is a theory of
    (A) fair trade
    (B) health and illness
    (C) medicines and their side effects
    (D) how to tell funny jokes
    (E) writing medical literature

37. In the seventeenth century, some people believe that if the humors were out of balance people
    (A) needed to eat chocolate
    (B) began to lose their sense of humor
    (C) became sick
    (D) lost some of their intelligence
    (E) became very angry

38. In line 43, "conundrum" is best defined as
    (A) similarities
    (B) contrasting conditions
    (C) an interesting theory
    (D) an interesting observation
    (E) a difficult problem

Critical Reading Passage G
adapted from the novel, The Adventures of Tom Sawyer
By Mark Twain

"TOM!"

No answer.

"TOM!"

No answer.

"What's gone with that boy, I wonder? You TOM!"

No answer.

The old lady pulled her spectacles down and looked over them about the room; then she put them up and looked out under them. She seldom or never looked *through* them for so small a thing as a boy; they were her state pair, the pride of her heart, and were built for «style,» not service—she could have seen through a pair of stove-lids just as well. She looked <u>perplexed</u> for a moment, and then said, not fiercely, but still loud enough for the furniture to hear:

"Well, I lay if I get hold of you I'll—"

She did not finish, for by this time she was bending down and punching under the bed with the broom, and so she needed breath to punctuate the punches with. She resurrected nothing but the cat.

"I never did see the beat of that boy!"

She went to the open door and stood in it and looked out among the tomato vines and "jimpson" weeds that <u>constituted</u> the garden. No Tom. So she lifted up her voice at an angle calculated for distance and shouted:

"Y-o-u-u TOM!"

There was a slight noise behind her and she turned just in time to seize a small boy by the slack of his roundabout and arrest his flight.

"There! I might 'a' thought of that closet. What you been doing in there?"

"Nothing."

"Nothing! Look at your hands. And look at your mouth. What is that truck?"

"I don't know, aunt."

"Well, I know. It's jam—that's what it is. Forty times I've said if you didn't let that jam alone."

"My! Look behind you, aunt!"

The old lady whirled round, and snatched her skirts out of danger. The lad fled on the instant, scrambled up the high board-fence, and disappeared over it.

His aunt Polly stood surprised a moment, and then broke into a gentle laugh.

"Can't I never learn anything? Ain't he played me tricks enough like that for me to be looking out for him by this time? But old fools is the biggest fools there is. Can't learn an old dog new tricks, as the saying is. But my goodness, he never plays them alike, two days, and how is a body to know what's coming? He appears to know just how long he can torment me before I get my dander up, and he knows if he can make out to put me off for a minute or make me laugh, it's all down again."

Critical Reading

39. In line 9, the narrator describes that Aunt Polly wears glasses for
  (A) no reason
  (B) seeing better
  (C) fashion
  (D) catching Tom
  (E) appearing wealthy

40. The passage states in line 35 that Aunt Polly "stood surprised a moment, and then broke into a gentle laugh." This shows she is
  (A) amused
  (B) annoyed
  (C) unable to see clearly
  (D) uncertain
  (E) uncomfortable

41. In this passage, Tom might best be characterized as
  (A) innocent
  (B) dangerous
  (C) daring
  (D) mean-spirited
  (E) mischievous

42. When Aunt Polly catches Tom, she realizes he has
  (A) been stealing form the neighbors
  (B) tormenting the cat
  (C) mocking her behind her back
  (D) making her a present
  (E) been hiding in the closet eating jam

43. In line 19, "constituted" means
  (A) encircled
  (B) blocked
  (C) contrasted
  (D) made of
  (E) found

44. This passage suggests that Aunt Polly
  (A) will never forgive Tom
  (B) is used to Tom's tricks
  (C) doesn't like Tom
  (D) is a hard-working woman
  (E) has no conscience

45. In this passage, Aunt Polly seems to act as a/an
  (A) friend to Tom
  (B) parental figure to Tom
  (C) enemy to Tom
  (D) contrast to Tom
  (E) co-conspirator to Tom

46. In line 37, Aunt Polly says, "but old fools is the biggest fools there is." Who is she referring to?
  (A) Tom's parents
  (B) herself
  (C) the cat
  (D) Tom
  (E) her husband

Kweller Prep

Writing Assignment

New York City may be a tourist attraction, but it is a city that many people call home. Whether it's the beautiful parks or the busy downtown streets, there is some part of the city that ever New York City native loves the most.

Write an essay that describes what you consider to be the most interesting place to visit in New York City. Your essay should include descriptive details about that location that would help persuade visitors and tourists to visit that location. Your location can be any place that a visitor could and would want to go see. Your descriptions should include vivid detail that help to bring that location to life in the reader's mind, as well as to help them understand why it is worth visiting.

Your task is to create an overall portrait of that location that would persuade a non-resident or new visitor to New York City to consider adding that location to their trip itinerary.

You must write an essay in which you:

- Detailed descriptions about a specific location in New York City
- The type of activities that can be done there
- The specific reasons why visitors might enjoy that location
- Create a vivid understanding of that location in the reader's mind

MATHEMATICS

47. Evaluate the following: 24.496 × 0.0025
    (A) 0.006124   (B) 0.06124   (C) 0.6123   (D) 24.4985   (E) 171.472

48. How much greater is the sum of $2\frac{3}{4} + 1\frac{3}{8}$ than the quotient of $2\frac{3}{4} \div 1\frac{3}{8}$?
    (A) $\frac{1}{6}$ (B) $\frac{11}{32}$ (C) 2   (D) $2\frac{1}{8}$ (E) $4\frac{1}{8}$

49. There are 120 vehicles in a parking lot. The ratio of cars to trucks is 3:1. The next day there are 28 more vehicles in the lot, but the percentage of cars is the same. How many cars are in the lot on the second day?
    (A) 75   (B) 88   (C) 111   (D) 118   (E) 148

50. A pair of shoes at one store normally costs $65.75 but is $20% off. Another store has the same shoes but is offering 25% off. What is the maximum price the shoes can normally be at the second store so that after the discount they are less expensive than at the first store?
    (A) $49.31   (B) 52.60   (C) $70.12   (D) $70.13   (E) $72.23

51. Abigail is using blocks to build a tower. The blocks are 3 inches, 4 inches and 8 inches tall. She has stacked 3 blocks. How many different heights are possible for the tower?
    (A) 6   (B) 9   (C) 10   (D) 16   (E) 2

52. A dog weighs the same as 10 guinea pigs. A cat weighs the same as 7 guinea pigs. How many dogs will be equal in weight to 40 cats?
    (A) 5.7   (B) 17   (C) 23   (D) 26   (E) 28

53. If the pattern continues in the following table, which column will contain the letter "J"?

1	2	3	4	5
A	B	-	C	-
-	D	-	-	-
E	-	-	-	-

(A) 1 (B) 2 (C) 3 (D) 4 (E) 5

54. The Stanton family has three children. The average age of the children and their mother is 16. The average age of the children and their father is 15. How much older is Mrs. Stanton compared to Mr. Stanton?

(A) 1 year (B) 2 years (C) 3 years (D) 4 years (E) 5 years

55. Which design in Pattern B will have the same number of lines as the 15th design in Pattern A?

Pattern	Design #1	Design #2	Design #3	Design #4
A	△	◸◹	▽ in △	(4 small triangles)
B	□	□□	L-shape (3 squares)	(4 squares)

(A) 5 (B) 7 (C) 9 (D) 10 (E) 11

56. Austin took a surfing lesson for $25.00 and then paid an additional $9.50 per hour to rent a surf board during his weeklong vacation. At the end of the week his bill was $101. How many total hours did Austin rent the surfboard during the week?

(A) 6.5 (B) 7 (C) 7.5 (D) 8 (E) 9

57. Derek has $\frac{1}{2}$ as many baseball cards as Stephen. Evan has 12 more than $\frac{1}{5}$ of the number of cards Derek has. What is the minimum number of cards that all three have together?

(A) 15 (B) 26 (C) 28 (D) 34 (E) 46

Mathematics

58. The water from a large bucket that is $\frac{3}{4}$ full is poured into a smaller bucket. It fills the bucket $2\frac{1}{2}$ times. If the smaller bucket holds $1\frac{1}{2}$ gallons of water, how many gallons of water does the larger bucket hold?

    (A) 2 (B) $2\frac{4}{5}$ (C) $4\frac{3}{4}$ (D) 5 (E) $5\frac{1}{2}$

59. How many different ways can you express 82 as the sum of two even whole numbers? Zero does not count as an even number. Changing the order of the numbers does not count as a new sum.

    (A) 20 (B) 21 (C) 23 (D) 26 (E) 28

60. In a book with 110 pages, how many page numbers will include a 5 and be divisible by 3?

    (A) 7 (B) 8 (C) 10 (D) 11 (E) 17

61. What is the value for the following expression? $\dfrac{\frac{3}{8} - \frac{5}{16}}{1\frac{1}{4}}$

    (A) $\frac{1}{20}$ (B) $\frac{1}{16}$ (C) $\frac{5}{64}$ (D) $\frac{1}{8}$ (E) $1\frac{5}{16}$

62. What is the smallest number that can be multiplied by 155 that will result in a product that is even and divisible by 15 and 21?

    (A) 21 (B) 30 (C) 42 (D) 105 (E) 315

63. Grant bought an old bike, fixed it up, and sold it for 25% more than he paid for it. The new owner left the bike in the driveway where it got run over by the family car. He sold it for scrap metal and got $3, which was 2% of what he paid for it. How much did Grant buy the bike for originally?

    (A) $112 (B) $120 (C) $130 (D) $260 (E) $600

64. Drake and Marcus use their hands to measure the length of a table? The table length is eight Drake hands plus six Marcus hands long. If the length of one Drake hand is 2 cm more than a Marcus hand and the overall length of the table is 240 cm, what is the length of one Drake hand?

   (A) 16 cm   (B) 16.3 cm   (C) 17.1 cm   (D) 18 cm   (E) 18.2 c

65. A bakery makes cakes with a radius of 10 cm or 20 cm. Both cakes are placed into square boxes when purchased. How many more square centimeters are in the base of the box for the larger cake than the smaller cake?

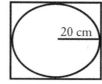

   (A) 100 cm²   (B) 300 cm²   (C) 800 cm²   (D) 1,000 cm²   (E) 1,200 cm²

66. A snow globe factory packs 12 snow globes in a box, and 8 boxes in a case to ship to stores. Which number of snow globes can be packed into boxes and fill the cases without any leftover?

   (A) 1,864   (B) 2,370   (C) 2,880   (D) 4,824   (E) 4,996

67. Students numbered 1 through 50 are standing in a line. A teacher goes through and pulls out students with numbers that are multiples of 2. Another teacher goes through and pulls out students with numbers that are multiples of 3. Assuming a teacher can select any multiple, what is the fewest number of additional teachers needed before all of the remaining students have prime numbers or the number 1?

   (A) 1   (B) 2   (C) 3   (D) 4   (E) 28

68. Joey can't remember the password for his phone. He does remember that it was a one digit number, followed by a vowel (A, E, I, O, U), followed by a one digit number. He also knows that the digits were not the same. How many different password combinations are possible?

   (A) 23   (B) 25   (C) 200   (D) 450   (E) 50

Mathematics

69. Two bunnies are 20 feet apart. They begin hopping toward each other. One bunny moves one foot forward each time it jumps. The other bunny is strong but timid and moves three feet forward but then scurries back one foot each time it jumps. How many feet apart are the two bunnies after each has jumped (and scurried back) 5 times?

(A) 5   (B) 6   (C) 8   (D) 9   (E) 10

70. Each of the shapes shown below represents a different number. The same shape always represents the same number. What is the value of the star?

  and

(A) 4   (B) 5   (C) 6   (D) 7   (E) 8

71. A floor that is 8 feet x 10 feet is covered by tiles that are 6 inch squares. How many fewer tiles would it take to cover the floor if the tiles were 12 inch squares?

(A) 80   (B) 160   (C) 220   (D) 240   (E) 320

72. Bella read 200 pages over 5 days. Each day, she read 10 pages more than the day before. How many pages did she read the first day?

(A) 10   (B) 12   (C) 20   (D) 28   (E) 40

73. What is the largest 5 digit number in which no digits are repeated and no digits are prime?

(A) 98,765   (B) 98,654   (C) 98,678   (D) 98,643   (E) 98,640

74. How many two digit numbers have digits that are not in ascending consecutive order?

(A) 80   (B) 82   (C) 90   (D) 91   (E) 92

75. A rectangular table is 1.5 times longer than it is wide. If the width was increased by 2 feet and the length remained the same, the table would be square. How many feet wide is the table?

(A) 2 (B) 3 (C) 4 (D) 6 (E) 8

76. Alice can clean a house in two hours. Her younger brother takes three hours to clean the house. How many hours would it take them to clean the house together?

(A) 1:12 (B) 1:20 (C) 2:15 (D) 2:30 (E) 2:45

77. If a bird randomly landed on the square sidewalk design shown, what is the probability that it would land on the darkest portion?

(A) 0.125 (B) 0.25 (C) 0.5 (D) 0.625 (E) 0.75

78. Olivia has 6 coins totaling 0.50 in her pocket. How many different coin combinations are possible?

(A) 1 (B) 2 (C) 3 (D) 4 (E) 5

79. During a winter storm Denver received twice as much snow as Boston. New York received the same amount as Boston and Denver combined. Both Detroit and Cleveland received less snow than Boston. Which city received the most snow?

(A) Boston (B) Cleveland (C) Denver (D) Detroit (E) New York

80. What number is in the ones digit of the product of 22 9s?

(A) 1 (B) 4 (C) 7 (D) 8 (E) 9

81. What is the difference between the smallest number divisible by all of the single odd digits and the smallest number divisible by all of the single even digits? Zero is not odd or even.

(A) 24 (B) 291 (C) 315 (D) 339 (E) 921

ANSWER EXPLANATIONS FOR PRACTICE TEST 1
ENGLISH LANGUAGE ARTS

1. Choice C is correct. Throughout the passage, the narrator describes images of running in the grass, wading through water, sticking feet out of the hot covers in winter, and leaping over fences. Each of these images convey a sense of freedom and each is associated with a new pair of shoes.

2. Choice C correct. When Douglas mentions that the shoes feel like "iron," he means they weigh him down, unlike the new shoes that would allow him to leap and run freely.

3. Choice C is correct. When Douglas walks by the store window where he sees the shoes, he is immediately transfixed or captivated. The reader knows this because as he walks by, "his ankles seized, his feet suspended, then rushed…. Douglas walked backward, watching the tennis shoes." It is almost as if Douglas is drawn to the shoes and seeing them holds him in place, fully occupying his attention.

4. Choice D is correct. When Douglas' mother asks about the movie, his only reply is "It was…" He trails off before even completing his sentence. The reader can assume that this is because he's so involved in looking at the shoes that he can't really think of anything else in that moment.

5. Choice D is correct. Douglas tries to explain the "magic" of the shoes to his father. However, all his father can say is "What's wrong with last year's sneakers?" This shows the lack of understanding between father and son.

6. Choice A is correct. The refraction that the narrator describes causes a visual distortion. We know this because he says how this refraction causes you to "[see] your feet below [the water], half an inch further downstream… than the real part of you above water." In other words, the distortion creates an optical illusion where your feet seem to be in a different place than the rest of you.

7. Choice C is correct. In particular, the narrator says Douglas "felt sorry for the boys who lived in California where they wore tennis shoes all year and never knew what it was to get winter off your feet." In other words, because boys in California live in temperate weather all year and never have to wear heavy winter shoes, they can appreciate what its like to finally be able to "peel off" the heavy shoes of winter. Douglas' joyous experience would be lost on them.

8. Choice A is correct. Throughout this passage, the narrator presents some very vivid imagery when Douglas is thinking of the shoes, including how they have "marshmallows and coiled springs in the soles" and that they are woven with grasses. These descriptions are so vivid and imaginative that they makes the reader see tennis shoes—something completely ordinary—in a way they never had before. This, in turn, speaks to Douglas' own imaginative powers.

9. Choice B is correct. To do something with haste means to do it quickly or in a rush.

10. Choice E is correct. The mood of this passage is suspenseful. As Morris tells his tale, his audi-ence members lean in closer, wanting to hear more of his story which, in turn, makes the reader feel that same sense of suspense. Additionally, there are some questions surrounding the monkey's paw, like why the first man who had the paw wished for death, why Morris throws the paw onto the fire, and why Morris warns them of the consequences of using the paw. All of these questions remain unanswered, leaving the reader in suspense.

11. Choice C is correct. "Presumptuous" means arrogant. Herbert's question to Morris about whether or not he has made a set of wishes is a bold, prying question.

12. Choice A is correct. "Wary" means to show caution. For reasons unknown to the reader, Morris warns the White family against using the paw, suggesting using the paw could have less-than- desirable consequences. He even throws the paw into the fire, showing that he doesn't want the family to use the paw. All around, he seems cautious when it comes to using the paw.

13. Choice A is correct. When Morris first starts telling his story the "three listeners leaned forward eagerly." In this case, this action suggests that that are intrigued by his story.

Answer Explanations For Practice Test 1

14. Choice C is correct. We know that Mr. White is curious about the paw because he has many questions about it. Additionally, he is the one who snatches the paw off the fire, suggesting that he wants to find out how it works for himself.

15. Choice D is correct. If someone does something because it suits their fancy, it's on a whim or impulse. You may have been tempted to select E, highly decorative, because this is another meaning of the word "fancy." However, in the context of this sentence, this is not the correct answer.

16. Choice B is correct. When Sylvia first encounters the young man in paragraph 1, the text says she is "horror-stricken" and she goes to hide in the bushes. Both of these details communicate her fear.

17. Choice B is correct. If something is "inaudible," it means that it difficult to hear. Sylvia speaks this way in this portion of the passage as a result of her fear.

18. Choice B is correct. You may have heard the phrase a "gallant knight" before. The word conjures images of chivalrous, brave, and mannerly knights. The young man here speaks gallantly because he's being polite to Sylvia, despite her fear of him.

19. Choice E is correct. We know that Mrs. Tilley is referring to the old cow here because, after calling the cow an "old trial," she asks Sylvia, "Where'd she tuck herself away this time, Sylvy?" Because of this, the reader knows that she is not talking to Sylvia, and she is certainly not talking to the young man. The only other entity present is the cow.

20. Choice C is correct. The young man tells Sylvia in line 11, "I have been hunting for some birds… and I have lost my way."

21. Choice D is correct. As soon as Mrs. Tilley meets the young man, she welcomes him into her home, telling him that he can make himself at home. The narrator also says that her "slumbering hospitality seemed to be easily awakened." Someone who is "hospitable" is welcoming to guests.

22. Choice E is correct. Something that is "shrouded" is wrapped up. In the context of this story, the room is hung with so many black tapestries that it seems all wrapped up. Answer choice B may have been a tempting answer, as the draperies are so extravagant that they do almost hide the walls; however, that is not what "shrouded" means.

23. Choice C is the correct answer. To have a profusion of something is to have a large quantity of it.

24. Choice D is the answer. The text says "a heavy tripod, bearing a brazier of fire… projected its rays on the tinted glass." Because of this, you might have been tempted to select choice C, "a heavy tripod." However, the brazier isn't a heavy tripod because it is born by (i.e. "bearing") or *sitting on* the tripod. Instead, we know that a fire is burning within the brazier, so we can assume it's some kind of container for holding coals or fire.

25. Choice E is correct. The room might be considered frightening because of all the details that describe it. The panes of the windows are described as "blood-red," which immediately invokes feelings of death or harm. Additionally, the brazier produces shadows that were "ghastly in the extreme," or horrifying. Immediately when people enter this room they take on a "wild look" and few are "bold" or brave enough to enter the room. Each of these descriptions conveys to the reader that this is a frightening place.

26. Choice E is correct. Whenever someone's countenance is described, it means their face or their facial expression.

27. Choice B is correct. The text describes how, each time the clock chimes on the hour, "the orchestra were constrained to pause" and "the waltzers perforce ceased their evolutions." It is as if, for a moment, everything stops and time stands still.

28. Choice E is correct. The text says that "the musicians… made whispering vows, each to the other, that the next chiming of the clock should produce in them no similar emotion." We know from details before this that the clock caused the whole party to stop and caused confusion and unease—this is the "emotion" referred to in this quote. So, the musicians are vowing that the clock will not catch them off guard the next time it chimes.

29. Choice D is correct. In the first two stanzas, the author uses words like "cheered," "merrily," "bright" and "sun." Each of these words evokes positive feelings and, thus, the mood is cheerful.

Kweller Prep

Answer Explanations For Practice Test 1

30. Choice A is correct. The text says, "And now the STORM-BLAST came, and he / was tyrannous and strong." This is an example of personification, where the narrator is making the storm cloud seem as if it is alive. Choice C may have thrown you off because the sun is personified in this manner as well, but line 9 specifically references the storm.

31. Choice C is correct. Each of these words makes the ice seem threatening—things that roar and howl and growl are often some kind of scary animal, and the ice is portrayed in this same sort of way.

32. Choice B is correct. The text says the storm is "tyrannous and strong." The word tyrannous is usually used to describe a leader who is too powerful, and strong is a synonym for powerful.

33. Choice C is correct. The text mentions a "dismal" sheen from the ice, meaning gloomy. A sheen is basically a cast of light or something shining, so though the word "bright" in choice D is related to the shine, this isn't what "dismal" means. You may have also been tempted to mark choice B, dangerous, because the ice certainly is dangerous. However, that again is not the best definition for "dismal."

34. Choice B is correct. The answer to this question is in line 4. The author talks about how in the seventeenth century hot chocolate, tea, and coffee were brought to Europe for the first time. She states, specifically, "they were classified at first not as food, but as drugs."

35. Choice D is correct. The word "impassioned" contains the word "passion," which means strong feelings, so we can conclude that an "impassioned warning" has some sort of strong feelings behind it.

36. Choice B is correct. The author says in line 33, "Humoralism, a theory of health and illness…"

37. Choice C is correct. The author states in line 38 that when humors were balanced, "they maintained a healthy functioning of an organism. When the balance among them tipped and one occurred in excess, it produced symptoms of what we now call 'disease in the body.'" Disease is, of course, another way to say that someone became sick.

38. Choice E is correct. The author states that some treatises faced a "conundrum" regarding the nature of chocolate. This means they faced a difficult problem in deciding whether or not chocolate was actually dangerous.

39. Option C is correct. We know that Aunt Polly only uses her glasses as a sort of fashion accessory because the author says they were "built for 'style' not service." Additionally, the narrator comments, that "she could have seen better through a pair of stove-lids just as well," suggesting just how non-functional they are.

40. Option A is correct. Laughter is typically associated with amusement. The fact that Aunt Polly laughs at Tom, despite his mischief, suggests that she is amused by his antics.

41. Option E is correct. In this passage, we learn several things about Tom: he often pulls pranks on his aunt, he has been hiding from her in a closet, and he ate the jam that she specifically asked him not to eat. Mischievous is a word used to describe someone who makes mischief, or trouble, and Tom is certainly fits that description.

42. Option E is correct. The key to this answer is in line 24 and line 28. Aunt Polly says to Tom, "I might 'a' thought of that closest. What you been doing in there?" and then "It's jam—that's what it is. Forty times I've said if you didn't let that jam alone."

43. Option D is correct. "Constitute" means "made of something." Since the garden is "constituted" of weeds, it's made up solely of weeds.

44. Option B is correct. The key to this question lies in the last paragraph of this passage. In talking to herself, Aunt Polly asks, "Ain't he played me tricks enough like that for me to be looking out for him by this time?" This seems to suggest that Tom is constantly pulling these sort of pranks on Aunt Polly and that she is used to it.

45. Option B is correct. Throughout this passage, Aunt Polly does seem like a parental figure to Tom. Like a parent would, she scolds him for eating the jam when she has especially told him not to. It also seems as though she is trying to keep him out of trouble.

46. Option B is correct. In the last paragraph of this passage, Aunt Polly is talking to herself, calling herself a fool for constantly falling prey to Tom's trickery.

ANSWER EXPLANATIONS FOR PRACTICE TEST 1

WRITING ASSIGNMENT

Although many people visit New York City every year, most only go to the most travelled places. Times Square, Wall Street and Central Park get thousands of visitors almost every day. Any visitor to New York City should also consider visiting some lesser known, but much more interesting locations. One such place is Highland Park. Any visitor to New York City who wants to see art and nature should add Highland Park to their list of places to see.

Highland Park has many different pieces of artwork that cannot be found in anywhere else in New York City. Located in the park is one amazing tribute to the soldiers who died in World War I. Called the "Dawn of Glory", the statue is of a male figure disrobing. The dark color of the statute makes anyone who sees it feel both sad and proud, as well as thankful for the soldiers who have served and died for the country.

Any visitor to New York City who loves gardens should make sure that Highland Park is on their itinerary. The park is home to a Children's Garden. The garden is a community garden, and is maintained by local children, their families and the community. It is filled with beautiful plants and flowers, and is an example of how communities work together in New York City to create and maintain a connection to nature.

Highland Park was recently upgraded, and now has gorgeous walking paths through woods and beside a reservoir. There are benches to sit and relax, where you can enjoy the sights and the sun. Nature lovers can also enjoy a quick walk or run through the park's beautiful setting.

Although New York City has a lot of big and popular places to visit, there are some locations that are quieter and more peaceful. Highland Park is one of those places. It may not be the most popular location, but it is a park filled with art, nature and history. It is one of the largest parks in New York City, and a quiet, lovely place to visit for anyone who wants to enjoy a quieter, more peaceful part of New York City.

ANSWER EXPLANATIONS FOR PRACTICE TEST 1
MATHEMATICS

47. Answer B is correct. To multiply decimals, first multiply the values as if they were whole numbers. Then count the number of digits behind the decimal point in the original numbers and place the decimal point so that the product has the same number of digits behind the decimal. $24{,}496 \times 25 = 612{,}400$. After the decimal is moved 7 places to the left, the result is 0.06124.

48. Answer D is correct. Turn both values into improper fractions of $\frac{11}{4}$ and $\frac{11}{8}$ to find the sum and the quotient. Using a common denominator of 8 to find the sum results in $4\frac{1}{8}$. To find the quotient, multiply by $\frac{8}{11}$ which is the reciprocal of $\frac{11}{8}$. The quotient is 2. "How much greater" means to find the difference, so $4\frac{1}{8} - 2 = 2\frac{1}{8}$.

49. Answer C is correct. The ratio of cars to truck is 3:1, so the ratio of cars to total vehicles is 3:4, which means 75% of the vehicles are cars. The total cars on the second day is 148 and 75% of 148 is 111.

50. Answer C is correct. The cost of the shoes at the first store can be found by using the equation $65.75 \times 0.8 = 52.60$. The equation $52.6 \div .75 = 70.13$ is used to determine 75% of what cost will be the same price as the shoes at the first store. The maximum price the shoes can be is the value closest to $70.13, which is $70.12.

51. Answer C is correct. The possible 3 block combinations are:
All one size: (3, 3, 3), (4, 4, 4), (8, 8, 8)
Two of one size plus one different: (3, 3, 4), (3, 3, 8), (4, 4, 3), (4, 4, 8), (8, 8, 3), (8, 8, 4)
All 3 different: (3, 4, 8)
Since none of the combinations will result in the same height, all 10 possible combinations count.

52. Answer E is correct. Dividing the dog's weight by 10 & the cat's weight by 7 will make them both equal to one guinea pig, and therefore equal to each other. $\frac{d}{10} = \frac{c}{7}$. By using cross multiplication we get $7d = 10c$. Since 40 cats is 4 times greater than 10 cats, we can multiply both sides of the equation by 4 to determine the number of dogs, which is 28.

53. Answer A is correct. The pattern is that initially zero boxes are skipped between letters and as each additional letter is added, one additional box is skipped. You could solve the problem by counting out the pattern. Or you could think of it mathematically.

Letter	A	B	C	D	E	F	G	H	I	J
Boxes Skipped		0	1	2	3	4	5	6	7	8

The number of boxes skipped for each additional letter is always two less than the number of the letter. The total number of boxes skipped to get to J is the sum of the number of boxes skipped to get to all of the letters, plus the number of boxes filled by the letters before J (9). $(8+7+6+5+4+3+2+1+9=45)$ Since there are 5 columns, the 45th space will fall on column 5. J will fall on the 46th space, which is in column 1.

54. Answer D is correct. The average of the 3 kids and their mother is 16, so the total of their ages is $16 \times 4 = 64$. The average of the 3 kids and their father is 15, so the total of their ages is $15 \times 4 = 60$. The difference between the two is 4.

55. Answer D is correct. Pattern A starts with 3 lines and adds 2 lines each time. The total number of lines for a given design can be found by multiplying the design number by 2 and adding 1. Pattern B starts with 4 lines and adds 3 lines each time. The total number of lines for a given design can be found by multiplying the design number by 3 and adding 1. The 15th design of Pattern A will have 31 lines ($15 \times 2 + 1 = 31$). The 10th design of Pattern B will also have 31 lines ($10 \times 3 + 1 = 31$).

56. Answer D is correct. To find the total that Austin spent on rental fees, subtract the cost of the lesson from the total (101 − 25 = 76). Divide 76 by 9.50 to find the number of hours that he rented the surfboard, which is 8.

57. Answer C is correct. The most important clue is that Evan has $\frac{1}{5}$ the number of cards Derek has plus 12 more. This means that the fewest number of cards that Derek could have is 5, otherwise $\frac{1}{5}$ of his total would be less than one card. If Derek has 5 cards, that means Stephen has 10 cards. Evan has 13 cards ($5 \times \frac{1}{5} + 12$). The total is 28 cards (5 + 10 + 13 = 28).

58. Answer D is correct. To find the total number of gallons that was poured out of the bucket multiply the amount the smaller bucket holds by the number of times it was filled ($1\frac{1}{2} \times 2\frac{1}{2} = 3\frac{3}{4}$). Divide this amount by how full the larger bucket was to determine how many gallons it can hold if full ($3\frac{3}{4} \div \frac{3}{4} = 5$).

59. Answer A is correct. There are 41 pairs of numbers that have a sum of 82 before they start repeating. For example 2 + 80 is the same as 80 + 2. The last pair before the pairs begin to repeat is 41 + 41, which can be eliminated because both numbers are odd. This leaves 40 pairs of numbers. Half these number pairs are made up of odd numbers and can be eliminated, leaving 20 pairs.

60. Answer A is correct. The page numbers that include a 5 and are a multiple of 3 will be multiples of 15 that include a 5: 15, 45, 75, and 105. The pages 51, 54, and 57 also include a 5 and are a multiple of 3, which brings the total to 7 pages.

61. Answer A is correct. Use a common denominator of 16 to subtract the fractions in the numerator. Their difference is $\frac{1}{16}$. Multiply this by $\frac{4}{5}$, which is the reciprocal of $1\frac{1}{4}$. The result is $\frac{1}{20}$.

62. Answer C is correct. For a number to be divisible by 15 and 21, it must contain all of the prime factors of those numbers (3, 5, and 7). For a number to be even, it must contain a factor of 2. Since 155 already contains the factor 5, it needs to be multiplied by the remaining factors of 2, 3, and 7, which result in a product of 42.

63. Answer B is correct. The initial value of the bike multiplied by 1.25 and then multiplied by 0.02 results in a final value of $3. To find the initial value, use division to work backwards (3 ÷ (1.25 × 0.02) = 120)

64. Answer D is correct. It took a total of 14 hands to measure the length of the table. Eight of the hand lengths are each 2 cm longer than the other 6, which results in 16 additional (240 -16 =224) centimeters. Subtracting the additional centimeters (leaves the number of centimeters that were covered by 14 hand lengths. Divide the remaining centimeters by 14 hands to get the length of one Marcus hand (224 ÷ 14 = 16). Drake's hand =Marcus +2=18.

65. Answer E is correct. The radius of each cake is one half the length of one side of the square box. T e area of the base of the smaller box is 202. The area of the base of the larger box is is 402.
1,600
T 400 = 1,200 .

66. Answer C is correct. To be packed evenly into boxes and cases, the number of snow globes must be evenly divisible by 96, since each case holds 12 times 8 or 96 globes. Only C satisifes this need.

67. Answer B is correct. After the first 2 teachers go through eliminating students with numbers that are multiples of 2 or 3, the remaining numbers are 1, 5, 7, 11, 13, 17, 19, 23, 25, 29, 31, 35, 37, 41, 43, 47, and 49. To eliminate the remaining numbers that are not prime would require two more teachers: one selecting students with numbers that are multiples of 5 to eliminate 25 and 35; and one selecting students with numbers that are multiples of 7 to eliminate 49.

Answer Explanations For Practice Test 1

68. **Answer D is correct.** There are 10 possible digits for the first spot, 5 letter choices for the second spot, and 9 possible digits for the third spot (since a digit cannot repeat). To find the possible combinations, find the product ($10 \times 5 \times 9 = 450$).

69. **Answer A is correct.** For each jump the two bunnies make toward each other they get a total of 3 feet closer together. After 5 jumps each, they would have closed the gap by 15 feet. The original distance was 20 feet so, $20 - 15 = 5$.

70. **Answer E is correct.** Since $8^2 = 64$ and $4^2 = 16$ the pentagon in both expressions is equal to 6 and the oval in both expressions is equal to 4. This is the only squared single digit number that will meet these requirements.

71. **Answer D is correct.** The floor is 80 feet^2 (8×10). (Currently each square foot of the floor is covered by 4 tiles for a total of 320 tiles ($80 \times 4 = 320$). If the tiles were 12 inches on each side, each tile would cover one square foot and you would only need 80 tiles all together. To find the difference subtract ($320 - 80 = 240$).

72. **Answer C is correct.** If Bella read 10 more pages on the second day, she read $10 + 10$ more pages on the third day, $10 + 10 + 10$ more pages on the fourth day and $10 + 10 + 10 + 10$ more pages on the fifth day. The extra number of pages she read each day is 100. The remaining 100 pages should be divided evenly between the 5 days, which means she read 20 pages on the first day.

73. **Answer E is correct.** A prime number is a number with no factors other than one and itself. The only number that does not contain a prime number or repeating digits is 98,640.

74. **Answer B is correct.** There are 90 2 digit numbers. For each group of numbers that starts with 1 through 8 in the tens place, there is one number that is in consecutive order (12, 23, 34, 45, 56, 67, 78, and 89). To find the number that are not in consecutive order subtract ($90 - 8 = 82$).

75. **Answer C is correct.** If 2 feet are added to the width it will be the same as the length. Substitute different values into the equation $w + 2 = l$. For example, $2 + 2 = 4$. If the width is 2, the length is 4. This is not correct because the length also has to be 1.5 times the width and 4 is not . If 4 is substituted for the width the result is $4 + 2 = 6$. Since in this case the length is 1.5 times as long as the width, the width of the table must be 4 feet.

76. **Answer A is correct.** Alice cleans the house in 2 hours, meaning she cleans $\frac{1}{2}$ the house in one hour. Her brother cleans the house in 3 hours, which means he can clean $\frac{1}{3}$ of the house in one hour. Together, they could clean $\frac{5}{6}$ of the house in 1 hour. Since $\frac{5}{6}$ of the job requires 1 hour, the remaining $\frac{1}{6}$ of the job can be completed in $\frac{1}{5}$ of an hour, which is 12 minutes. The total time needed is 1 hour and 12 minutes.

77. **Answer B is correct.** The entire design could be covered with 8 triangles that are the shape and size of the existing dark triangles. Two of those triangles qualify as the darkest portion. Two out of eight is the same as 25% or 0.25.

78. **Answer B is correct.** Olivia could have 1 quarter and 5 nickels ($0.25 + (5 \times 0.05) = 0.50$) or 4 dimes and 2 nickels (($4 \times 0.1) + (2 \times 0.05) = 0.50$).

79. **Answer E is correct.** Detroit and Cleveland received less snow than Boston, putting them at the bottom of the list. Denver received twice as much as Boston, so Denver has so far received the most. However, New York received as much as Boston and Denver combined, moving it to the top of the list.

80. **Answer A is correct.** When you multiply 9s together, you quickly start to notice a pattern in the ones digit ($9 \times 9 = 81$), ($9 \times 9 \times 9 = 729$), ($9 \times 9 \times 9 \times 9 = 6,561$), ($9 \times 9 \times 9 \times 9 \times 9 = 59,049$). If the 9s are being multiplied an even number of times, the product ends in 1. If the 9s are being multiplied an odd number of times, the product ends in 9. Since 22 9s are being multiplied together, the product will end in 1.

Answer Explanations For Practice Test 1

81. Answer B is correct. For a number to be divisible by 3, 5, 7, and 9 it must contain the factors 5, 7, and 9. It does not need to contain the factor of 3, because any number that is a multiple of 9 will always be a multiple of 3. Since 5 × 7 × 9 = 315, this is the smallest number divisible by the odd single digit factors. For a number to be divisible by 2, 4, 6, and 8, it must contain the factors 3 and
8. It does not need to contain the factors of 2 or 4 because any number that is a multiple of 8 will be a multiple of 2 and 4. Since 3 × 8 = 24, this is the smallest number divisible by the even single digit numbers. The difference between the two is 291 (315 - 24 = 291).

Practice Test 2

Student's Name: _____   Admissions ID Code: _____

Student's Signature: _____   Date of Birth: _____

PRACTICE TEST 2 FOR HUNTER COLLEGE HIGH SCHOOL EXAMINATION

(THIS TEST WAS CREATED BASED ON A SAMPLE TEST PROVIDED BY HUNTER COLLEGE HIGH SCHOOL)

This test contains three sections: 47 multiple-choice **English Language Arts questions**, a **Writing Assignment**, and 35 multiple-choice **Mathematics questions**.

Each multiple-choice question is followed by **five possible answers: A, B, C, D, or E.** Choose the best answer for each question. You may make marks in this test booklet; use the space between questions and the blank pages in your booklet for scrap paper. **There is no penalty for guessing.**

On the answer sheet, carefully blacken the circle that contains the letter of the answer you select. Use only a Number 2 pencil for the multiple-choice sections. If you wish to change an answer, carefully erase the wrong answer completely and mark your new answer. **As soon as you finish one section of the test, go on to the next section. Monitor the time the proctor writes on the board.**

Calculators are not permitted.

You have a total of **three hours to complete the examination**, including the Writing Assignment.

If you complete the test before the time is up, review your previous work to correct for errors. Make sure that your answer sheet is accurately and cleanly prepared.

You may not remove any page from this booklet or take papers from the test room.

LANGUAGE ARTS
Critical Reading

Each of the following passages is followed by questions based on its content. Choose the letter of the answer that best reflects what is stated or implied in the passage.

Reading Passage A

Steve Tolman had done a wrong thing and he knew it. While his father, mother, and sister Doris had been absent in New York for a weekend visit, the boy had taken the car from the garage without anybody's permission and carried a crowd of his friends to Torrington to a football game. That was not the worst of it, either. At the foot of the long hill leading into the village, the car he had so unceremoniously borrowed had come to a halt, refusing to move another inch, and Steve now sat helplessly in it, awaiting the aid his comrades had promised to send back from the town.

Steve scowled with disappointment. The catastrophe served him right. Unquestionably he should not have taken the car without asking. He had never driven it all by himself before, although many times he had driven it when his father had been with him. It had gone all right then. What reason had he to suppose a mishap would befall him now?

Goodness only knew what was the matter with the thing. Probably something was smashed, something that might require days or even weeks to repair, and would cost a lot of money. How angry his father would be!

The boys had not given him much sympathy, either. They had been ready enough to egg him on into wrong-doing, but the moment fun had been transformed into calamity, they had deserted him with incredible speed, climbing out and trooping off on foot to town. It was easy enough for them to wash their hands of the affair and leave him to the solitude of the roadside; the automobile was not theirs and when they got home they would not be confronted by irate parents.

Language Arts

1. Steve's car trip proved to be a disaster primarily because
   (A) he got in a car accident
   (B) his parents came home early from New York and found out he had stolen the car
   (C) his friends did not offer to help him
   (D) the car broke down unexpectedly
   (E) the car had a history of engine problems

2. In the second paragraph, the author implies that Steve
   (A) had never driven a car before
   (B) always obeyed his parents
   (C) was good at handling emergency situations
   (D) did not have a driver's license
   (E) felt no guilt over taking the car

3. The author implies that Steve's friends pressured him to
   (A) drive the car too fast
   (B) join them for a football game he didn't want to attend
   (C) ask his father to borrow the car
   (D) walk to town with them
   (E) steal the family car

4. As used in line 17, "calamity" means
   (A) fortune
   (B) chaos
   (C) disaster
   (D) calm
   (E) sadness

5. Steve experienced the "solitude of the roadside" (line 19) because
   (A) he was left home alone
   (B) he had been the only one in the car that day
   (C) he was not invited to the football game
   (D) his friends abandoned him
   (E) his was the only car on the road

6. Steve believed that the reason his friends did so little to help him with his problem was that
   (A) they knew nothing about how to repair a car
   (B) they did not care about Steve
   (C) they weren't the ones who would be in trouble
   (D) they weren't involved in the car theft
   (E) they couldn't miss the football game

7. As used in line 19, "irate" means
   (A) angry
   (B) jealous
   (C) disappointed
   (D) proud
   (E) missing

Reading Passage B
How the Leaves Came Down

"I'll tell you how the leaves came down,"
The great Tree to his children said:
"You're getting sleepy, Yellow and Brown,
Yes, very sleepy, little Red.
5   It is quite time to go to bed."

"Ah!" begged each silly, pouting leaf,
"Let us a little longer stay;
Dear Father Tree, behold our grief!'
It's such a very pleasant day,
10   We do not want to go away."

So, for just one more merry day
To the great Tree the leaflets clung,
Frolicked and danced, and had their way,
Upon the autumn breezes swung,
15   Whispering all their sports among—

"Perhaps the great Tree will forget,
And let us stay until the spring,
If we all beg, and <u>coax</u>, and fret."
But the great Tree did no such thing;
20   He smiled to hear their whispering.

"Come, children, all to bed," he cried;
And ere the leaves could urge their prayer,
He shook his head, and far and wide,
Fluttering and rustling everywhere,
25   Down sped the leaflets through the air.

I saw them; on the ground they lay,
Golden and red, a huddled swarm,
Waiting till one from far away,
White bedclothes heaped upon her arm,
30   Should come to wrap them safe and warm.

The great bare Tree looked down and smiled.
"Good-night, dear little leaves," he said.
And from below each sleepy child
Replied, "Good-night," and murmured,
35   "It is *so* nice to go to bed!

Language Arts

8. This poem is used primarily as a way to explain
   (A) why leaves change colors in the fall
   (B) that animals hibernate in winter
   (C) why snow falls in the winter
   (D) why trees lose their leaves in autumn
   (E) that trees feel human-like emotions

9. After the leaves begged the Tree to stay with them (stanza 2), the Tree
   (A) immediately shed all of the leaves
   (B) told the leaves they could stay on for the winter
   (C) allowed the leaves to remain for only one more day
   (D) covered the leaves in snow
   (E) told the leaves they didn't need to go to sleep

10. As used in line 18, "coax" means
    (A) call
    (B) persuade
    (C) ignore
    (D) yell
    (E) sleep

11. When the author speaks about someone coming with "white bedclothes upon her arm," she is referring to
    (A) a woman who has been doing laundry
    (B) a child using her bed sheet as a shield against the wind
    (C) a gardener come to rake up the fallen leaves
    (D) a white oak tree falling to the ground
    (E) the fall of winter snow

12. In the end, the leaves are content because
    (A) they know they can return to the tree someday
    (B) they are happy to be raked into a pile together
    (C) they think it is cozy to be covered with snow
    (D) the tree allows them to stay on its branches
    (E) they understand why the seasons change

Reading Passage C

Beverly is an old town and not especially progressive. It has little attractiveness for strangers. Beverly contains several beautiful old residences, however, built generations ago and still surrounded by extensive grounds where the trees and shrubbery are now generally overgrown and neglected. One of these fine old places, the most imposing residence in the town, had been leased some two years ago by Colonel James Weatherby, whose family consisted of his widowed daughter, Mrs. Burrows, and his grandchild, Mary Louise Burrows.

Colonel Weatherby was a man of exceptionally distinguished appearance, tall and dignified, with courtly manners and an air of prosperity that impressed the simple villagers with awe. His snow-white hair and piercing dark eyes, his immaculate dress upon all occasions, the whispered comments on his ample deposits in the local bank, all contributed to render him remarkable among the three or four hundred ordinary inhabitants of Beverly, who, after his two years' residence among them, scarcely knew him. Colonel Weatherby was an extremely reserved man and seldom exchanged conversation with his neighbors. In truth, he had nothing in common with them and even when he walked out with Mary Louise, he merely acknowledged the greeting of those he met by a dignified nod of his stately head.

With Mary Louise, however, he would converse fluently and with earnestness, whether at home during the long evenings or on their frequent walks through the country, which were indulged in on Saturdays and holidays during the months that school was in session and much more often during vacations. The Colonel owned an automobile, which he only drove on rare occasions. Colonel Weatherby loved best to walk and Mary Louise enjoyed their tramps together because Grandpa Jim always told her so many interesting things and was such a charming companion. He often developed a strain of humor in the girl's company and would relate anecdotes that made her laugh. Yes, Grandpa Jim was really funny, when in the mood.

He was fond of poetry, too, and the most severe trial Mary Louise was forced to endure was when he carried a book of poems in his pocket and insisted on reading from it while they rested in a shady nook by the roadside or on the bank of the little river that flowed near by the town. Mary Louise had no soul for poetry, but she would have endured far greater hardships rather than forfeit the companionship of Grandpa Jim.

13. The description of the town as having "little attractiveness to strangers" (lines 1-2) helps to emphasize that
    (A) Colonel Weatherby was considered an outsider in Beverly
    (B) the inhabitants of Beverly were all unhappy
    (C) there were no benefits to living in a small town like Beverly
    (D) all of the homes in Beverly were in poor condition
    (E) Mary Louise did not want to move to Beverly

14. In the passage, James Weatherby is referred to as "The Colonel" until line 22. After that, he is called "Grandpa Jim." The author uses this name change because
    (A) at that point in the story, James became a grandfather
    (B) the more informal name shows that James was beloved in the town
    (C) it provides contrast between James' warm relationship with Mary Louise and his otherwise distant nature
    (D) James preferred an informal tone when conversing with his neighbors
    (E) it shows the special relationship James had with Mary Louise, his only remaining family member

15. Colonel Weatherby rarely talked to others in the town because
    (A) he did not enjoy conversation
    (B) he felt he had nothing in common with them
    (C) he was intimidated by their superior wealth
    (D) they knew too much about him, which made him uncomfortable
    (E) they were rude to his daughter

16. Mary Louise frequently listened to her grandfather read poems because
    (A) she shared his love of poetry
    (B) she enjoyed his company, no matter the subject
    (C) she felt obliged to spend time with him
    (D) she hoped it would improve her own writing
    (E) she wanted to spend time with him but knew he was not skilled at conversation

17. Mary Louise and her grandfather took walks together
    (A) only during vacations from school
    (B) because it was their only means of transportation
    (C) as frequently as possible
    (D) without ever stopping to rest
    (E) so that he could make her listen to his poems

18. As used in line 13, "seldom" means
    (A) often
    (B) earnestly
    (C) quietly
    (D) rarely
    (E) happily

19. Colonel Weatherby's sense of humor
    (A) was difficult to appreciate
    (B) was evident to everyone he met
    (C) was very dry
    (D) was most present in his poems
    (E) emerged in the company of his granddaughter

20. The townspeople's reaction to Colonel Weatherby can best be described as
    (A) admiration
    (B) indifference
    (C) condescension
    (D) anger
    (E) bitterness

21. As used in line 29, "forfeit" means
    (A) endure
    (B) receive
    (C) continue
    (D) ignore
    (E) give up

22. Many of the villagers perceive Colonel Weatherby as
    (A) funny
    (B) mysterious
    (C) poor
    (D) spry
    (E) friendly

Reading Passage D

Elizabeth Ann's Great-aunt Harriet was a widow who was not very rich or very poor, and she had one daughter, Frances. When Elizabeth Ann's father and mother both died when she was a baby, although there were many other cousins and uncles and aunts in the family, these two women fairly rushed upon the little baby-orphan, taking her home and surrounding her henceforth with the most loving devotion.

They had really given themselves up to the new responsibility, especially Aunt Frances, who was very conscientious about everything. As soon as the baby came there to live, Aunt Frances stopped reading novels and magazines, and re-read one book after another which told her how to bring up children, and she joined a Mothers' Club which met once a week. So you can see that by the time Elizabeth Ann was nine years old Aunt Frances must have known all that anybody can know about how to bring up children, and Elizabeth Ann got the benefit of it all. She loved the little girl with all her heart, and longed, above everything in the world, to protect her from all harm and to keep her happy and strong and well.

Yet Elizabeth Ann was neither very strong nor well. She was very small for her age, with a rather pale face and big dark eyes which had in them a frightened, wistful expression that went to Aunt Frances's tender heart and made her ache to take care of Elizabeth Ann better and better.

Aunt Frances said once to a visiting lady, "I have had her from the time she was a little baby and there has scarcely been an hour she has been out of my sight. But I do wish she weren't so thin and pale and nervous." To Elizabeth Ann she added, hastily, "Now don't go getting notions in your head, darling. Aunt Frances doesn't think there's anything *very* much the matter with you. You'll be all right again soon if you just take the doctor's medicine nicely. Aunt Frances will take care of her precious little girl. She'll make the bad sickness go away." Elizabeth Ann, who had not known before that she was sick, had a picture of herself lying in the little white coffin, all covered over with white. In a few minutes Aunt Frances was obliged to excuse herself from her visitors and devote herself entirely to taking care of Elizabeth Ann.

One day, Aunt Frances really did send for the doctor. Elizabeth Ann was terribly afraid to see him, for she felt in her bones he would say she would die before the leaves cast a shadow. Elizabeth Ann, when she first stood up before the doctor, had been quaking with fear lest he discover some deadly disease in her, but after thumping her and looking at her lower eyelid inside out, and listening to her breathing, he pushed her away with a little jerk and said, "There's nothing in the world the matter with that child."

Of course, Aunt Frances didn't let him off as easily as that. She fluttered around him as he tried to go, and she said all sorts of things to him, like "But, Doctor, she hasn't gained a pound in three months ... and her sleep ... and her appetite ... and her nerves ..."

The doctor said back to her, as he put on his hat, all the things doctors always say under such conditions, "Plenty of fresh air ... more sleep ... She'll be all right ..." but his voice did not sound as though he thought what he was saying amounted to much.

Just then, something happened which changed Elizabeth Ann's life forever and ever. It was a very small thing, too. Aunt Harriet coughed. Aunt Harriet had been coughing like that ever since the cold weather set in, for three or four months now, and nobody had thought anything of it because they were all so much occupied in taking care of the sensitive, nervous little girl who needed so much care; and yet, at the sound of that little discreet cough behind Aunt Harriet's hand, the doctor whirled around and <u>fixed</u> his sharp eyes on her, with all the bored, impatient look gone, the first time Elizabeth Ann had ever seen him look interested. "What's that? What's that?" he said, going over quickly to Aunt Harriet. He snatched out of his little bag a shiny thing with two rubber tubes attached, and he put the ends of the tubes in his ears and the shiny thing up against Aunt Harriet, who was saying, "It's nothing, Doctor… a little teasing cough I've had this winter."

The doctor motioned her very impolitely to stop talking, and listened very hard through his little tubes. Then he turned around and looked at Aunt Frances as though he were angry at her. He said, "Take the child away and then come back here yourself." In the few days which followed, the family talked over the doctor's verdict, which was that Aunt Harriet was very, very sick.

23. Upon taking Elizabeth Ann into their home as a baby, Harriet's and Frances' feelings can best be described as
    (A) reluctance
    (B) self-confidence
    (C) determination
    (D) bitterness
    (E) indifference

24. Aunt Frances stopped reading magazines
    (A) in order to spend all of her time playing with Elizabeth Ann
    (B) because Harriet told her they were a waste of time
    (C) so that Elizabeth Ann wouldn't see them
    (D) to read parenting books instead
    (E) because her eyesight was poor due to her illness

25. Elizabeth Ann first thought that she might be sick when
    (A) she went to see the doctor
    (B) Aunt Harriet told her she looked pale
    (C) she noticed that she was very small for her age
    (D) she fainted in the hallway
    (E) she overheard Aunt Frances tell someone that she was sick

26. Although Aunt Frances' words to Elizabeth Ann (lines 19-22) were meant to be _____, in fact, they were _____ to Elizabeth Ann.
    (A) serious; funny
    (B) reassuring; frightening
    (C) sympathetic; rude
    (D) callous; comforting
    (E) informative; confusing

27. Elizabeth Ann was "quaking with fear" (line 28) at the doctor's office because
    (A) she was scared about what would happen to Aunt Harriet
    (B) visits to the doctor always made her nervous
    (C) she was afraid the examination would hurt
    (D) she had convinced herself that she was dying
    (E) Aunt Harriet had told her that she was very sick

28. As used in line 20, "notions" means
    (A) ideas
    (B) desires
    (C) objections
    (D) convictions
    (E) aches

29. Aunt Frances' initial reaction to the doctor was one of

(A) anger
(B) acceptance
(C) trust
(D) disbelief
(E) gratitude

30. The doctor's diagnosis was surprising because

(A) Aunt Harriet had shown no prior signs of illness
(B) no one expected Elizabeth Ann to be sick
(C) everyone had been too preoccupied with Elizabeth Ann to worry about Harriet
(D) the doctor was unqualified to give this opinion
(E) Aunt Frances was confident she knew exactly what was wrong with Elizabeth Ann

31. As used in line 43, "fixed" means

(A) closed
(B) repaired
(C) focused
(D) averted
(E) prepared

Reading Passage E

Katy Carr lived in the town of Burnet, which wasn't a very big town, but was growing as fast as it knew how. The house she lived in stood on the edge of the town. It was a large square house, white, with green blinds, and had a porch in front, over which roses and clematis made a thick bower. Four tall locust trees shaded the gravel path which led to the front gate. On one side of the house was an orchard; on the other side were wood piles and barns. Behind that was a garden sloping to the south, and behind that a pasture with a brook, butternut trees, and four cows.

There were six of the Carr children—four girls and two boys. Katy, the oldest, was twelve years old; little Phil, the youngest, was four, and the rest fitted in between. Dr. Carr, their Papa, was a dear, kind, busy man, who was away from home all day, and sometimes all night, too, taking care of sick people. The children hadn't any Mamma. She had died when Phil was a baby. Katy could remember her pretty well; to the rest she was but a sad, sweet name.

In place of this Mamma, whom they recollected so dimly, there was Aunt Izzie, Papa's sister, who came to take care of them when Mamma went away on that long journey, from which, for so many months, the little ones kept hoping she might return. Aunt Izzie was a small woman, sharp-faced and thin, rather old-looking, and very neat and particular about everything. She meant to be kind to the children, but they puzzled her much, because they were not a bit like herself when she was a child. Aunt Izzie had been a gentle, tidy little thing, who loved to sit and to have her head patted by older people and be told that she was a good girl; whereas Katy tore her dress every day and didn't care a button about being called "good," while Clover and Elsie shied off like restless ponies when any one tried to pat their heads. It was very perplexing to Aunt Izzie. Then Dr. Carr was another person who worried her. He wished to have the children hardy and bold and encouraged climbing and rough play, in spite of the bumps and ragged clothes which resulted.

32. Which of these was NOT found on the Carr's property?
   (A) A white house
   (B) Livestock
   (C) A brook
   (D) A horse
   (E) An orchard

33. Katy is **different** from her siblings because she is the only one who
   (A) likes to play outside
   (B) is well-behaved
   (C) remembers her mother
   (D) likes Aunt Izzie
   (E) takes care of the cows

34. It was important to Dr. Carr that Aunt Izzie come to stay with the family because
   (A) Aunt Izzie was wonderful with children
   (B) he feared Aunt Izzie would be lonely otherwise
   (C) he needed someone to help out temporarily while his wife was on a trip
   (D) he thought she would provide the children with much-needed discipline
   (E) he had to work so often

35. The author uses the phrase "long journey" (line 14) to indicate
    (A) a vacation that Mrs. Carr took
    (B) the trip Aunt Izzie made from her old home to live with the Carrs
    (C) the hard time that Aunt Izzie had in learning to live with the children
    (D) Mrs. Carr's death
    (E) Dr. Carr's long struggle with grief

36. Dr. Carr and his sister disagreed about
    (A) whether or not she should live with the family
    (B) the value of education
    (C) the importance of obedience in children
    (D) the long hours that Dr. Carr worked
    (E) how roughly children should be allowed to play

37. As used in line 22, "perplexing" means
    (A) confusing
    (B) predictable
    (C) surprising
    (D) reasonable
    (E) irritating

38. Based on the information in the passage, Katy can best be described as
    (A) timid
    (B) independent
    (C) well-mannered
    (D) self-conscious
    (E) cooperative

Reading Passage F

The little old lady lived over the way, through a green gate that shut with a click, and up three white steps. Every morning at eight o'clock the church bell chimed for Morning Prayer and every morning at eight o'clock the little old lady came down the white steps, and opened the gate with a click, and went where the bells were calling.

About this time also little Ida would kneel on a chair at her nursery window in the opposite house to watch the old lady come out and go. The old lady was one of those people who look always the same. Every morning her cheeks looked like faded rose-leaves, and her white hair like snow. Every morning she wore the same black satin bonnet and the same white shawl, had delicate gloves on the smallest of hands, and gathered her skirt daintily up from the smallest of feet. Every morning, whatever the weather might be, she stood outside the green gate, and looked up at the sky to see if this were clear, and down at the ground to see if that were dry; and so went where the bells were calling.

Ida knew the little old lady quite well by sight, but she did not know her name. She made up a name for the little old lady herself, however, and called her Mrs. Overtheway. Morning after morning, though breakfast smoked upon the table, she would linger at the window, beseeching, "One minute more! Please let me wait until Mrs. Overtheway has gone to church." When the little old lady had come out and gone, Ida would creep from her perch, and begin her breakfast.

It had been a quiet amusement, demanding no exertion, to see what little she could see of the old lady's life, and to speculate about what she could not; to wonder and fancy what Mrs. Overtheway looked like without her bonnet, and what she did with herself when she was not at church. Ida's imagination did not carry her far. She believed her friend to be old, immeasurably old, indefinitely old; and had a secret faith that she had never been otherwise. She felt sure that she wore a cap indoors; that she helped herself at meals, and went to bed according to her own pleasure and convenience; was—perhaps on these very grounds—utterly happy, and had always been so. This was one of many things which formed the attraction for Ida in the little old lady who lived over the way. That green gate shut in a life of which the child knew nothing, and which might be one of mysterious delights; to believe that such things could be was consoling, and to imagine them was real entertainment.

39. At eight o'clock each morning
    (A) Ida ate breakfast
    (B) Mrs. Overtheway visited Ida
    (C) Mrs. Overtheway left for church
    (D) church bells rang to signal the end of a service
    (E) Ida woke up

40. Ida enjoyed watching Mrs. Overtheway because
    (A) it was comforting to imagine the old woman's happy life
    (B) Mrs. Overtheway had always been kind to her
    (C) the old woman's daily routine was very interesting
    (D) Mrs. Overtheway was an old family friend
    (E) Mrs. Overtheway was unpredictable

41. As used in line 18, "beseeching" means
    (A) wondering
    (B) worrying
    (C) forgetting
    (D) pleading
    (E) obeying

42. According to the passage, Mrs. Overtheway was
    (A) a widow
    (B) spontaneous
    (C) a name Ida invented
    (D) unfriendly
    (E) a relative of Ida

43. Based on the information in the passage, Ida can best be described as
    (A) outgoing
    (B) imaginative
    (C) obedient
    (D) helpful
    (E) fearful

44. Which of these is a fact about Mrs. Overtheway rather than an assumption that Ida makes about her?
    (A) She goes to bed whenever she wants.
    (B) She is happy.
    (C) She eats a lot.
    (D) She wears a black bonnet when she is inside.
    (E) She attends church daily.

45. As used in line 32, "consoling" means
    (A) strange
    (B) fascinating
    (C) comforting
    (D) joyous
    (E) disconcerting

46. When author mentions Ida's "secret faith" (line 26), it shows
    (A) how Ida and Mrs. Overtheway share religious beliefs
    (B) Ida's vivid imagination
    (C) the truth of Mrs. Overtheway's life
    (D) the limits of a child's understanding
    (E) Ida's loneliness

47. Ida's feelings toward Mrs. Overtheway can best be described as
    (A) detachment
    (B) dependence
    (C) indifference
    (D) mutual
    (E) affection

Writing Assignment

New York City is a unique and gigantic city where millions of people learn to live in peace with one another. Each day, New Yorkers walk past thousands of other people. Some of those people might need help if they are having a bad day.

Write an essay or tell a true story about a time when you saw a person being kind to another. Describe a time when you saw someone help another just because it was the right thing to do. You might write about a person lending money for the subway, someone helping a person to cross a busy street, someone allowing another to get in front of them in line if they are in a hurry, or a time when you saw a person help give directions to someone who was lost. These are just some examples of the kindness and help that New Yorkers give each other every day. What have you seen?

Your task is to create a story about a helpful event you witnessed. Use sensory details (the five senses: sight, sound, smell, touch, and taste) to describe the event you saw. In this essay, you must answer the following:

- Did this event happen to you personally or did you watch this happen?
- Where and when did this event occur?
- Why did this person need help?
- How was this person helped?
- How did this event make you feel?
- Is it important for people to help others? Why or why not?

MATHEMATICS

48. Evaluate the following: 12.8234 − 2.9927
 (A) 9.8310 (B) 9.9307 (C) 8.9907 (D) 9.8302 (E) 9.8307

49. If twice the average of 5.12 and 4.83 is multiplied by 0.67, the result is:
 (A) 6.67 (B) 9.95 (C) 7.69 (D) 6.76 (E) 6.66

50. What is the value of $\left(\frac{2}{5} \div \frac{1}{3}\right) \times \frac{1}{2}$?
 (A) $\frac{4}{8}$ (B) 1 (C) $\frac{3}{5}$ (D) $\frac{3}{2}$ (E) $\frac{3}{4}$

51. In lowest terms the sum of $\frac{1}{3}, \frac{3}{4}$ and $\frac{5}{12}$ is:
 (A) $\frac{1}{3}$ (B) $\frac{3}{2}$ (C) $\frac{8}{12}$ (D) $\frac{2}{7}$ (E) $\frac{3}{4}$

52. What is the value of the following expression? $\dfrac{\frac{2}{5} + \frac{1}{10}}{\frac{1}{6} + \frac{2}{3}}$
 (A) $\frac{7}{5}$ (B) $\frac{3}{5}$ (C) $\frac{2}{5}$ (D) $\frac{2}{9}$ (E) $\frac{1}{6}$

53. What is the 2014th digit in the repeating decimal 0.142857142857...
 (A) 4 (B) 7 (C) 1 (D) 8 (E) 5

54. The lumber yard charges 32 cents for the first yard of wood, and 18 cents for each additional yard. If you have $8.50, what is the greatest number of yards you could purchase?
 (A) 45 (B) 46 (C) 49 (D) 42 (E) 40

55. The top three students in the class scored 96%, 92%, and 91% respectively. If the average of the top four students is 93%, what did the fourth student score?
 (A) 90 (B) 91 (C) 92 (D) 93 (E) 94

Mathematics

56. A lily pad is growing on a 100 mile river at an increasing rate. On the first day the lily pad covers 2 miles, the second day 4 miles, and the third day 8 miles. In how many days will the river be completely covered?
(A) 7 (B) 12 (C) 8 (D) 11 (E) 4

57. Matt runs faster than Gabe, who runs twice as fast at Marie. Marie runs at half the rate of Sarah, but Sarah runs slower than Janice. Which of the following statements is true?
(A) The fastest person must be Matt.
(B) The fastest person must be Sarah.
(C) The slowest person must be Sarah.
(D) Neither Gabe nor Janice could be the fastest person.
(E) Either Matt or Janice must be the fastest person.

58. The rectangular wall below has a surface area of 70 feet. What percent of the surface area does the triangle cover?

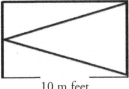

10 m feet

(A) 53% (B) 46% (C) 50% (D) 33% (E) 45%

59. When the average of the 21st even natural number and the 15th even natural number is added to the 7th odd natural number, what is the result? (The natural numbers are 1, 2, 3, 4, ...)
(A) 53 (B) 152 (C) 43 (D) 49 (E) 48

60. The digits in a two digit number sum to 8 and yield a product of 12. Which of the following answers could be the two digit number?
(A) 62 (B) 80 (C) 34 (D) 17 (E) 24

61. If Maddy has 12 pencils, 4 pens, and 8 markers, how many sets of 3 different writing instruments can she bring to school?
(A) 48 (B) 502 (C) 138 (D) 432 (E) 384

Kweller Prep

62. In this grid, the dots are spaced one unit apart, horizontally and vertically, creating square units. What is the number of square units enclosed by the shape?

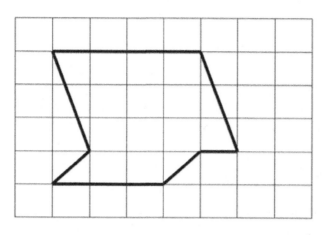

(A) 14 (B) 15 (C) 16 (D) 17 (E) 18

63. In the expression below, each letter represents a non-zero one-digit number. Where the same letter appears, it represents the same number in each case. Each distinct letter represents a different number. What number is represented by A?

$$A + B = 8$$
$$A + B = C + D$$
$$D - C = 2$$
$$A, B \text{ divisible by } 2$$

(A) 5 (B) 1 (C) 2 (D) 4 (E) 7

64. Malachi had a cold, and he accidentally got 5 friends sick. Each of those friends infected 4 other people, who in turn infected 2 people. To the nearest tenth, what percent of the sick people (not including Malachi) were the original 5 friends that Malachi got sick?

(A) 10.0% (B) 11.5% (C) 12.0% (D) 7.7% (E) 6.5%

65. Leslie wants to visit her dad in Florida. She can take 5 trains to the airport, 4 different flights to Florida, and 2 car services from the airport in Florida to her dad's house. How many ways can she get to her dad's house?

(A) 10 (B) 11 (C) 24 (D) 34 (E) 40

Mathematics

66. Caleb bought a model car for 80% of its original sales price. He lent it to Tony for 40% of what he paid, and Tony in turn lent it to Steven for 20% of what Tony paid. What percent of the original price did Steven pay for the car?

   (A) 2.00%   (B) 5.00%   (C) 0.09%   (D) 6.4%   (E) 0.20%

67. Amanda spent half of her babysitting money on a book that was on sale for 25% off the original price; at the sale price, she could have bought 3 books for $30. How much did Amanda make babysitting?

   (A) $13.33   (B) $26.67   (C) $37.11   (D) $26.00   (E) $15.55

68. How many squares are in this diagram?

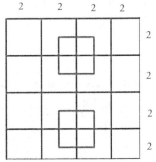

Not drawn to scale

   (A) 40   (B) 39   (C) 35   (D) 26   (E) 28

69. If a room measuring 9 feet by 12 feet is covered with carpet measuring 5 feet by 6 feet, what percent of the room is not covered by carpet?

   (A) 72.2%   (B) 68.3%   (C) 8.0%   (D) 27.8%   (E) 35.4%

70. When Brett and Taylor pulled weeds, they each earned $12.50 per hour. When they worked with Steph, they averaged $13.00 per hour. What is the amount the lawn owner saved by hiring all three kids for an hour instead of hiring Steph for three hours?

   (A) $4   (B) $3   (C) $9   (D) $1   (E) $5

71. In the diagram below, there are three right angles. In square cm, what is the total area?

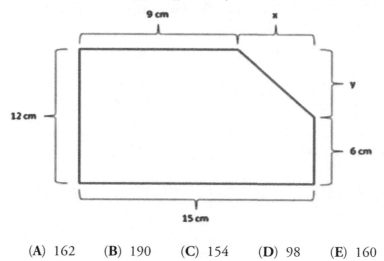

(A) 162 (B) 190 (C) 154 (D) 98 (E) 160

72. Name the four digit number ABCD that satisfies all of the following conditions:
  i. A, B, C, D are the numbers 1, 2, 4, and 8 each used once
  ii. AB is divisible by D
  iii. ABC is even
  iv. A + B < C + D

(A) 8412 (B) 1284 (C) 1428 (D) 2148 (E) 2418

73. All of the families can adopt either 1 or 2 pets. In total 15 birds were adopted, 14 cats were adopted, and 15 dogs were adopted. 6 families adopted birds and cats, 2 families adopted birds and dogs, and 4 families adopted cats and dogs. What percent of families adopted 2 pets?

(A) 30.5% (B) 35.5% (C) 37.5% (D) 28.0% (E) 35.0%

74. Five people enter a room, and each person shakes hands with every other person exactly once. How many handshakes occur?

(A) 15 (B) 12 (C) 14 (D) 16 (E) 10

75. Two trains are 260 miles apart. The first train starts at Point A and travels at 70 miles per hour, and the second train starts at Point B and travels toward Point A at 60 miles per hour. When the trains meet, how many miles away are they from Point B?

(A) 100 (B) 120 (C) 140 (D) 150 (E) 160

Mathematics

76. Melanie covers the outside of a 10 x 10 x 10 inch cube with a layer of 1 x 1 x 1 inch cubes. What is the surface area of the new cube in square inches?

   (A) 256   (B) 848   (C) 864   (D) 826   (E) 854

77. How many two digit whole numbers increase in value when their digits are reversed?

   (A) 20   (B) 23   (C) 26   (D) 29   (E) 36

78. Everyone bikes at the same speed. David biked for twice as much time as Melvin, who biked for one third as much time as Dan. If Dan rode 12 miles, how many miles did David ride?

   (A) 8   (B) 6   (C) 12   (D) 7   (E) 11

79. How many two digit whole numbers are divisible by 4 and 7?

   (A) 1   (B) 2   (C) 3   (D) 4   (E) 5

80. Megan counted her coin collection of dimes and quarters that added up to $4.00 total. If Megan drops one of her 31 coins, what is the probability that the coin is a dime?

   (A) 87.5%   (B) 80.6%   (C) 86.8%   (D) 88.6%   (E) 80.8%

81. The football coach wants to divide up the players for group practice. If he makes groups of 3, no one is left out. If he makes groups of 4, 3 athletes are left out. If he makes groups of 5, some students are left out. There are fewer than 50 athletes. How many people are on the team?

   (A) 17   (B) 19   (C) 27   (D) 23   (E) 28

82. Mikey plans to make 4 x 4 inch greeting cards from a piece of cardstock that measures 24 by 13 inches. What is the maximum number of squares that he can cut out?

   (A) 16   (B) 15   (C) 27   (D) 21   (E) 18

Kweller Prep

ANSWER EXPLANATIONS FOR PRACTICE TEST 2
ENGLISH LANGUAGE ARTS

1. Option D is correct. In line 5, the text states, "the car he had so unceremoniously borrowed had come to a halt, refusing to move another inch, and Steve now stat helplessly in it, awaiting the aid his comrades had promised to send back from the town." Here, it is clear that the car has unexpectedly broken down, stranding Steve.

2. Option D is correct. The second paragraph mentions that Steve had never driven the car without his father before and that he had never driven it all by himself. This suggests that Steve probably doesn't have his driver's license yet.

3. Option E is correct. The key to this answer lies in line 15, when the narrator states, that his friends "had been ready enough to egg him on into wrong-doing." The "wrong-doing" referred to here is taking the car without his parents' permission.

4. Option C is correct. A calamity is best defined as a disaster. For Steve, this experience is a calamity because it seems like everything has gone wrong for him.

5. Option D is correct. In the final paragraph of this passage, Steve laments the fact that his friends have abandoned him. For this reason, he feels a sense of solitude, or a feeling of aloneness.

6. Option C is correct. At the end of the passage, the narrator states of the friends, "the automobile was not theirs and when they got home they would not be confronted by irate parents." In other words, the friends don't seem to care about Steve's plight because they aren't the ones who are going to be in trouble.

7. Option A is correct. "Irate" means angry.

8. Option D is correct. This poem tells the story about how leaves fall from the trees. You may have been tempted to mark Option A; however, the poem doesn't really offer an explanation of how the colors change, though it does mention leaves who are Yellow and Brown.

9. Option C is correct. The poem states in line 11 "So, for just one more merry day/ To the great Tree the leaflets clung." In other words, the Tree allowed the leaves to hang on to him for one more day.

10. Option B is correct. To "coax" something means to gently persuade.

11. Option E is correct. This is an example of personification, in which something non-human (winter) is de-scribed as if it were human.

12. Option C is correct. The winter snow falling on the leaves is described as pleasant "bedclothes" that wrap the leaves "safe and warm." This would suggest that the leaves are content to be cozily covered with snow.

13. Option A is correct. This statement suggests that there are few outsiders in Beverly. As a result, the emphasizes that Colonel Weatherby is indeed an outsider because there aren't many people like him.

14. Option C is correct. In shifting from "The Colonel" to "Grandpa Jim," the author changes the reader's perception of him as a character. While he may seem distant and formal as "the colonel" to others in the community, he is the endearing "Grandpa Jim" to Mary Louise.

15. Option B is correct. The text states in line 15, "In truth, he had nothing in common with them."

16. Option B is correct. In the last sentence of this selection, the narrator states, "Mary Louise had no soul for poetry, but she would have endured far greater hardships rather than forfeit the companionship of Grandpa Jim." This suggests that, even if she doesn't share his love of poetry, she enjoys his companionship.

17. Option C is correct. The text states in line 19 that Mary Louise and Grandpa Jim took "frequent walks."

18. Option D is correct. The word "seldom" means "rarely" or "infrequently."

Answer Explanations For Practice Test 2

19. Option E is correct. Line 25 states that Grandpa Jim "often developed a strain of humor in the girl's company and would relate anecdotes that made her laugh. Yes, Grandpa Jim was really funny, when in the mood." This shows that Grandpa Jim really does have quite a sense of humor when in the presence of his granddaughter.

20. Option A is correct. The text states in line 10, "his immaculate dress upon all occasions, the whispered comments on his ample deposits at the local bank, all contributed to render him remarkable among the three or four hundred ordinary inhabitants of Beverley." The inhabitants of the town, even though they don't know much about the Colonel, clearly admire him and think him "remarkable."

21. Option E is correct. To "forfeit" something means to give it up.

22. Option B is correct. Though the villagers admire Colonel Weatherby from a distance, they don't really know much about him. For this reason, he seems quite mysterious.

23. Option C is correct. Harriet and Francis seem quiet determined once they take in Elizabeth Ann. This is evident in details such as how Frances stops reading novels and magazine, and joined a Mother's club.

24. Option D is correct. The passage says in line 8, "Aunt Frances stopped reading novels and magazines, and re-read one book after another which told her how to bring up children." Instead of reading things for pleasure, Aunt Frances begins to read books how to raise a child instead.

25. Option E is correct. In the fourth paragraph, the author describes an incident in which Aunt Frances tells a visiting friend that that she "doesn't think there is anything very much wrong with [Elizabeth Ann.] The narrator goes on to say, "Elizabeth Ann, who had not known before that she was sick, had a picture of herself lying in a little white coffin…" Before overhearing her aunt's word's Elizabeth Ann has no notion at all that she might be sick.

26. Option B is correct. Though Aunt Francis tells Elizabeth Ann not worry, she immediately begins to worry, even picturing herself in a coffin.

27. Option D is correct. That Elizabeth Ann has convinced herself that is dying is evident in line 27 when the narrator says, "She felt in her bones [the doctor] would say she would die before the leaves cast a shadow."

28. Option A is correct. To have a "notion" about something is have an idea.

29. Option D is correct. When the doctor states that there is nothing wrong with Elizabeth Ann, Aunt Frances immediately protests, saying "But, Doctor, she hasn't gained a pound in three months.. and her sleep.. and her appetite.. and her nerves…" All of this shows that she does not believe the doctor's diagnosis.

30. Option C is correct. Throughout the passage, everyone is quite concerned with Elizabeth Anne's health and there is no indication that there actually might be something wrong with Aunt Harriet.

31. Option C is correct. If someone "fixes" their eyes on you, it means that they are focused on you.

32. Option D is correct. The first paragraph of the story provides a description of the Carr's property, but a horse is not included in this description.

33. Option C is correct. In line 13, the narrator says, "Katy could remember [her mother] pretty well; to the rest she was a sad, sweet name." In this quotation, "the rest" refers to the rest of the Carr children. Of all six of them, Katy is the only one who can remember her mother.

34. Option E is correct. Because Dr. Carr has to work so often, someone needs to care for the children. For this reason, he has his sister come live with them.

35. Option D is correct. The reader realizes after reading this passage that the mother has passed away. However, the "long trip" is a way for Dr. Carr to explain the mother's absence to his children.

36. Option E is correct. In the last paragraph of this passage, the narrator conveys the idea that Aunt Izzie had been a "gentle, tidy thing" as a child. This is contrasted to the more energetic and rough Carr children, whom Dr. Carr "wished to have… hardy and bold." These details reveal that they have different ideas about how the children should be allowed to play.

Answer Explanations For Practice Test 2

37. Option A is correct. Something that is "perplexing" is confusing.
38. Option B is correct. Because Katy "tore her dress every day and didn't care a button about being called 'good,'" she likely tends to do whatever she wants, independent of what her aunt or the other children think. The state of her dress also suggests that she is out seeking adventure or playing rough, not staying at home like her meek, well-behaved aunt would have as a child.
39. Option C is correct. This is revealed in line 2 of the passage which states, "Every morning at eight o'clock the church bell chimed for Morning Prayer and every morning at eight o'clock the little old lady came down the white steps, opened the gate with a click, and went to where the bells were calling."
40. Option A is correct. In the last paragraph of this passage, Ida images the life of Mrs. Overtheway. The narrator says that Ida felt sure Mrs. Overtheway was "utterly happy, and had always been so" in line 28.
41. Option D is correct. Beseeching means "pleading."
42. Option C is correct. According to line 16, Ida "made up a name for the little old lady herself, however, and called her Mrs. Overtheway."
43. Option B is correct. In this passage, especially the last paragraph, Ida imagines what Mrs. Overtheway's life is like, including what she does when she is inside her home and how she lives her life.
44. Option E is correct. This is the only option that is a fact; everything else is something that Ida has imagined. The first paragraph discusses how Mrs. Overtheway goes to church every day.
45. Option C is correct. Something that is "consoling" is "comforting."
46. Option D is correct. Ida believes whole-heartedly, with a consistent faith, that something impossible is true: Mrs. Overtheway has always been "indefinitely old." This, of course, is illogical because no one can be old for their entire life. Thus, this shows the limits of her child's understanding.
47. Option E is correct. Ida clearly feels affection for Mrs. Overtheway because of how she waits, every morning, to watch her go to church. She feels a sort of connection with her as she imagines the life she must have.

ANSWER EXPLANATIONS FOR PRACTICE TEST 2

Writing Assignment
(The Return)

Random acts of kindness happen in New York City. New Yorkers are friendly and kind and helpful people. We have become so helpful because we are forced to adapt to a life where people are around you all the time. My story is about a phone call, a windy day, and a homeless woman on the corner of W 58th and 9th Ave.

It was a cold autumn day. I saw a homeless woman curled up on the corner of a CVS store. The woman looked tired, cold, and sad. She was hugging herself and looking at her own kneecaps. We waited at the intersection for cars to pass.

Just then, a man walked by. The fast-walking man's phone rang, and, as he reached into his pocket, a bill fell out onto the ground. It immediately blew the bill past the woman on the corner. The woman saw the bill flying and she jumped up after it. She chased after the waving bill for half a block, snatched it up, and yelled, "Sir, your money!" she yelled over and over again. He walked back towards her, astonished as the woman handed him his money back. Just then, the man took the money and then immediately gave the money back to the woman. She was rewarded for doing the right thing.

I will always remember the look on the woman's face. Her eyes were large and watering, and her face looked frozen. The woman looked happy and surprised. I remember how she felt because I felt that way too. He probably thought that, if the woman didn't come after him, he would have lost the money anyway. That moment helped me see a person who knows right from wrong.

Seeing things like this happen in my neighborhood makes me feel fantastic. The woman didn't need to give the man his money. The man kept walking. He would never have known that the woman kept it. We need events like this in our city. We need people to help one another and to look out for each other.

ANSWER EXPLANATIONS FOR PRACTICE TEST 2
MATHEMATICS

48. The answer is E. To evaluate this expression, subtract 2.9927 from 12.8234, making sure to line up the decimal places correctly. You will have to calculate this by hand as there are no calculators allowed. Make sure to "borrow" correctly in the respective decimal places for 12.8234 so you can subtract the larger digits in 2.9927.

49. The answer is A. First, make sure you understand each piece of the problem. Calculate twice the average of 5.12 and 4.83. To get the average, add 5.12 and 4.83 to get 9.95, then divide by two to get the average of 4.975. We need to get "twice the average." This means taking 4.975 and multiplying by two, or for students who see a shortcut, not dividing the original 9.95 by two at all. Either way, you get 9.95 for "twice the average." Then multiply this value, 9.95, by 0.67. When you do this multiplication by hand, note that the answer, 6.6665, is not an exact match. You'll have to round this to the nearest answer choice, which is 6.67.

50. The answer is C. The first step here is to look at the fractions inside the parentheses. We know that dividing by a fraction is the same as multiplying by the reciprocal, so we can rewrite the beginning as:

$$\left(\frac{2}{5} \times \frac{3}{1}\right)$$

Well, that's the same as:

$$\left(\frac{2}{5} \times 3\right)$$

For the numerator, we get 6; for the denominator, we get 5. The result so far is

$$\left(\frac{6}{5}\right)$$

We are not done yet – now we have to multiply by one half.

$$\left(\frac{6}{5} \times \frac{1}{2}\right)$$

Note that we can reduce here: 6 is divisible by 2, so we can rewrite this as:

$$\left(\frac{3}{5} \times \frac{1}{1}\right)$$

This gives the final answer of three-fifths.

51. The answer is B. We need to add these fractions and then simplify the final answer. Let's start by converting everything into twelfths.

$$\left(\frac{1}{3} \times \frac{4}{4}\right) = \frac{4}{12}$$

$$\left(\frac{3}{4} \times \frac{3}{3}\right) = \frac{9}{12}$$

Adding everything together, we get eighteen twelfths. That's more than one (twelve twelfths), so we know we have to simplify.

$$\left(\frac{18}{12}\right) = \left(\frac{3}{2}\right)$$

This gives us choice B.

52. The answer is B. To solve this, we will have to get a common denominator for the top and the bottom of this fraction. For the top, let's convert everything into tenths. Then

$$\left(\frac{2}{5} \times \frac{2}{2}\right) = \frac{4}{10}$$

Adding one tenth to this gives up five tenths, or one half. For the denominator, let's convert two-thirds into sixths.

$$\left(\frac{2}{3} \times \frac{2}{2}\right) = \frac{4}{6}$$

Answer Explanations For Practice Test 2

Now we have one half on top divided by five sixths. From the earlier problem, remember that dividing by a fraction is the same as multiplying by a reciprocal. We'll flip over the five sixths to get:

$$\left(\frac{1}{2} \times \frac{6}{5}\right) = \frac{6}{10} = \frac{3}{5}$$

53. The answer is D. This question can be overwhelming if you don't see the trick right away. Notice that the decimal repeats: 0.142857 then another 142857. This means the first digit is always 1, second is 4, third is 2, fourth is 8, fifth is 5, and sixth is 7. We can divide 2014 by 6 to get 335.6, so instead of counting all the way to 2014 and wasting time, we know that the 2014th digit has to be one of the digits we already listed. Let's multiply 6 by 335 to get 2010 – this corresponds to the "cycle" of digits closest to 2014. We know that 2010 corresponds to the sixth digit, so 2011 corresponds to the first, 2012 to the second, 2013 to the third, and 2014 to the fourth digit, or 8.

54. The answer is B. Let's take $8.50 and subtract the cost of the first yard of wood to get $8.18. Now we will have to divide $8.18 by $0.18 to see the number of additional yards purchased. We get 45.4 yards, but the question doesn't say we can buy parts of a yard. The answer should be the original one yard plus 45 additional yards. To check, add $0.32 and 45 * $0.18 to get $8.42. If we tried 46 additional yards, the total would be $8.60, and that's over the limit of $8.50. However, the answer is one yard + 45 additional yards, for a total of 46 yards.

55. The answer is D. This problem makes you think about how an average is calculated. To get the average, you add up all the values, divide by the number of things you're averaging, and get a result. Here we know the result and the number of scores, but not one particular score. We can set this up as:

$$\left(\frac{96 + 92 + 91 + ?}{4}\right) = 93$$

We will multiply both sides by four to get:

$$96 + 92 + 91 + ? = 372$$

Now subtract the numbers from the left and right sides to get:

$$? = 93$$

56. The answer is A. In order to answer this problem, you have to see the pattern. Each day, the lily pad doubles in size, and to cover the river the lily pad must reach 100 miles. If it reaches 8 miles on day 3, it will reach 16 on day 4, 32 on day 5, 64 on day 6, and 108 on day 7. This exceeds the river size of 100 miles, so the river will be completely covered on day 7.

57. The answer is E. To solve this problem, think about the question in steps, from the first sentence, we know:

Matt > Gabe > Marie (Gabe is twice as fast)

From the second sentence, we know that:

Janice > Sarah > Marie (half rate of Sarah)

We also know that Marie runs at half the rate of Sarah, but Gabe runs twice and fast as Marie – this means that Gabe and Sarah run at the same speed. While we do not know if Matt or Janice is faster, one of them must be the fastest person.

58. The answer is C. First, we need to remember that surface area for a flat shape like this triangle just means area of the shape. If the area of a rectangle is 70 feet and one side is ten feet, the remaining size must be seven feet (as 7 x 10 = 70). Now we need to remember the calculation for area of a triangle: one-half (base x height). This means one-half (7 x 10) or 35. Note that 35 is half of 70, so the triangle covers 50% of the shape.

59. The answer is D. First, find out what the different numbers here are. The even natural numbers are 2, 4, 6, 8, etc. The 21st even natural number would be (2 x 21) = 42; the 15th even natural number would be (2 x 15) = 30. The odd natural numbers are 1, 3, 5, 7, 9, 11, 13 – the 7th odd natural number is 13. Take the average of 42 and 30 to get 36, and then add 13 to get 49.

60. The answer is A. First, think about all the ways to make eight. 1+7, 7+1, 2+6, 6+2, 3+5, 5+3, 4+4. This means our possible numbers are 17, 71, 26, 62, 35, 53, and 44. The next clue says that the numbers yield a product of 12. The only two digit numbers on our list that multiply to twelve are 26 and 62. 62 is answer choice A, and 26 does not appear.

61. The answer is E. For these combination problems, we need to think about the number of possibilities for each type. There are 12 options for pencils, 4 options for pens, and 8 options for markers. All we need to do is multiply 12 x 4 x 8, which gives us 384.

62. The answer is B. For these counting shape problems, it is important to work in a strategic way. First, count all the full squares. That gives us a total of 11 whole squares. Now let's work down each row – notice that the triangles for each row form another square. The top row really has 4 squares, the second has 4 squares, the third has 4 squares, and the bottom rom has three squares. This gives us a new total of fifteen squares.

63. The answer is C. First, think of all the possibilities for A and B. We know that A + B = 8, so the possibilities are:

    A B
    1 7
    7 1
    2 6
    6 2
    3 5
    5 3
    4 4

    (but we know each letter represents a different number)
    The last clue tells us that A and B are divisible by 2, which cuts down our list to:

    A B
    2 6
    6 2

    We also know that A + B = 8 = C + D. Since each letter must be used only once, this means C + D = 8.

    C D
    1 7
    7 1
    3 5
    5 3

    The last clue says that D − C = 2. This is only true when D = 5 and C = 3, so 5 − 3 = 2. Thus we know that C = 3, D = 5, and A, B are 2 and 6 or 6 and 2. Looking at the answers, only C (2) fits for A based on what we know.

64. The answer is D. Malchi gets 5 people sick, so these 5 represent the first 'tier' of sick people. Each of thoese 5 infects 4 more, so the second 'tier' includes 20 people, Those 20 each get 2 more sick, so the last 'tier' of sick people has 40 more. Add 5 plus 20 plus 40 to get 65 total, of which 5 is 7.69%, rounded to 7.7%.

65. The answer is E. We will use the multiplication for combinations strategy again. 5 choices for trains, 4 for flights, and 2 car services give us 5 x 4 x 2, or 40.

66. The answer is D. This question has several parts we need to solve. We will pick a number to "plug in" for the original car price. It is all right to do this because the answer choice we're looking for is not the original car price, it's the percent that the last boy paid. Let's suppose that the original car price was $100. We know Caleb bought the car for 80% of its original price, and 80% x $100 is $80. Now we know that Tony got the car for 40% of what Caleb paid.
Since Caleb paid $80, we need to take 40% x $80 = $32 to get what Tony paid. Then Steven got the car for 20% of what Tony paid, which means we take 20% x $32 = $6.40. However, this is not the final answer. We need to figure out what $6.40 is as a percent of the original $100. To do this, we divide $6.40 by $100 to get 6.4%.

Answer Explanations For Practice Test 2

67. The answer is B. For this problem, we will work backwards to find out how much Amanda made babysitting. Alternatively, you could try each value for babysitting money from the answer choices and see which one comes to the right book value at the end. However, this can take longer, so it's a better strategy when you do not know how to approach a problem.

    The end of the problem says that when books were on sale for 25% off, Amanda could have gotten 3 books for $30 dollars. That just means she could have gotten 1 book for $10 during the 25% off sale. If $10 is the price of a book that is 25% off, it's really the same as saying 75% of the book price originally was $10. To get 100% of the book's cost, we will divide $10 by 75% to get $13.33. Now we can look back at the original question – Amanda spent half of her babysitting money on the book. If she spent $13.33 on the book, we multiply by two in order to get her whole babysitting amount, $26.67.

68. The answer is A. Again, in this geometry problem we need to use a methodical system for counting the different squares. First, let's count each individual shape. Each row has 4 squares, giving us a total of 16. There are 8 small interior squares, bringing the total to 24. Now we need to count squares made by combining other shapes. Those small interior squares can create two more squares, bringing the total to 26. Then we can combine the shapes into larger squares, again working around the shape in a methodical fashion. Adding all of these smaller shapes together brings us to 39 squares, but don't forget to count the entire diagram! The real total is 40.

69. The answer is A. To solve this problem, we need to find the area of the room and the area of the carpet. The area of the room is 9 x 12 = 108, and the area of the carpet is 5 x 6 = 30. To get the percent covered by the carpet, we take 30 divided by 108, which gives us 27.8%. However, the question wants the percent of the room NOT covered by carpet, which is the remaining 72.2% (because 72.2% plus 27.8% give us 100%).

70. The answer is B. First, we need to find out how much Steph would have made for three hours. We know all three kids together average $13 an hour, and the boys each make $12.50 an hour.

    $$\left(\frac{12.50 + 12.50 + ?}{3}\right) = 13$$

    We multiply both sides by 3 to get 12.50 + 12.50 + ? = 39, and then subtract the 12.50 and 12.50 from both sides to get $14, what Steph makes per hour. If the lawn owner had hired Steph for three hours, he would have paid $14 x 3 = $42.
    By hiring all three kids for an hour, the lawn owner paid $13 x 3 = $39. The difference between $42 and $39 is $3, the amount he saved.

71. The answer is A. First, we need to figure out what the "x" represents. Since we know one side of the shape is 15 cm, the other side, which is 9 cm + x cm, must also add up to 15 cm. The other side is 12 cm, so its opposing side is 6 cm + 6 cm for a total of 12 cm as well. This means x is 6 cm. Now let's think about how to get the total area. We will "cut" this shape into different pieces to make the multiplication easier. First, let's look at the 9 cm x 12 cm rectangle on the left. Here, the total area is 108 cm. Now, let's look at the 6 cm by 6 cm square on the bottom right. The area here is 36 cm.
    Finally, we have the upper right triangle. We figured out that x represents 6 cm and the other side is 6 cm, so we use the one half (base x height) triangle formula to get one half (6 x 6) = 18. Now we add up all the pieces: 108, 36, and 18 = 162 for the total area.

72. The answer is B. Here, we will look at the five answer choices and get rid of ones that don't fit the provided rules. Each of the answer choices has the values 1, 2, 4, and 8 used once. Now we have to check whether AB, the first two numbers, are divisible by D, the fourth number.
    For choice A, is 84 divisible by 2? Yes. For B, 12 is divisible by 4. For C, 14 is NOT divisible by 8, so it can't be a correct choice. For D, 21 is NOT divisible by 8. For E, 24 is divisible by 8. We are left with A, B, and E.

73. The answer is C. We know the total number of each type of animal adopted, so we can determine how many were adopted by a one pet family and how many were adopted by a two pet family. 15 birds were adopted, but 6 families adopted birds and cats, and 2 families adopted birds and dogs. 15 − 6 − 2 = 7 birds adopted by single pet families. For the 14 cats, 6 families adopted birds and cats, and 4 families adopted cats and dogs. 14 − 6 − 4 = 4 cats adopted by single pet families. Of the 15 dogs, 2 families adopted birds and dogs, and 4 families adopted cats and dogs: 15 − 2 − 4 = 9 dogs adopted by single pet families.

   Now we can add up the number of single pet families: 7 + 4 + 9 = 20. From the question, the number of two pet families is 6 + 2 + 4 = 12. To get the percent of two pet families, we divide 12 by the total, or 12 divided by 32. This gives us 37.5%.

74. The answer is E. First, let's think of the different people as letters: our five people are A, B, C, D, and E. When A enters the room, she shakes hands with B, C, D, and E. Then B shakes hands with C, D, and E. C has already shaken hands with A and B, so C must shake hands with D and E. Then D shakes hands with E, for a total of ten handshakes.

$$A - B\ C\ D\ E$$
$$B - C\ D\ E$$
$$C - D\ E$$
$$D - E$$

75. The answer is B. To solve this problem, let's think about the first hour. Before the trains move, they are 260 miles apart. After one hour, the first train has gotten 70 miles away from Point A, and the second train has moved 60 miles from Point B. This means the trains are now 130 miles apart. During the second hour, the first train moves another 70 miles from Point A, and the second train moves 60 miles from Point B. The trains meet exactly at the end of hour two. The first train is 140 miles from Point A, and the second train is 120 miles from Point B, which is choice B.

76. The answer is C. To solve this question, we need to think carefully. The quick answer is to assume that the new cube is 11 inches wide, but this is incorrect. Melanie covers the cube entirely, so the new cube will actually be 12 inches wide, 12 inches deep, and 12 inches tall. To get the surface area of a cube, we need to get the area of one side and multiply by 6, because a cube's surface area is really the same as six squares. One of these squares has an area of 12 x 12 = 144, so six of these squares will be 6 x 144 = 864.

77. The answer is E. The best way to approach this problem is to think of all the two digit numbers (numbers from 10 to 99), and look for a pattern. Starting with the 10s, we see that 12, 13, 14, 15, 16, 17, 18, and 19 will all increase in value when the digits are reversed (a total of eight switches).

20s: 23, 24, 25, 26, 27, 28, 39
30s: 34, 35, 36, 37, 38, 39
40s: 45, 46, 47, 48, 49
50s: 56, 57, 58, 59
60s: 67, 68, 69
70s: 78, 79
80s: 89
90s: none

   Now we can count up all the two digit numbers we selected: from the 10s, we get 8; from the 20s, we get 7; from the 30s, we get 6, and so on. The total is 8 + 7 + 6 + 5 + 4 + 3 + 2 + 1 = 36.

78. The answer is A. To solve this problem, we will think about each person in turn. David biked for twice as much time as Melvin:

$$\text{David's miles/time} = 2 \times \text{Melvin's miles/time}$$

Melvin biked for one-third as much time as Dan.

$$\text{Melvin's miles/time} = 1/3 \times \text{Dan's miles/time}$$

Now we see that Dan rode for 12 miles, and we know everyone bikes at the same speed.

Answer Explanations For Practice Test 2

79. **The answer is C.** To solve this problem, let's start thinking about the two digit numbers from 10-99. The pattern for numbers divisible by 4 are 12, 16, 20, 24, 28, 32, 36, 40, 44, 48, etc. See the pattern of the last digit: 2, 6, 0, 4, 8. For the numbers divisible by 7, we know that 14, 21, 28, 35, 42, 49, 56, 63, 70, 77, 84, 91, 98. Here the pattern is much longer, but still visible on the end digits. All we have to do is select the numbers appearing on both lists: this includes 28, 56, and 84.

80. **The answer is B.** At first, this problem could be overwhelming. Let's do a common sense check. We have 31 coins and we want them to add up to $4.00. If we have 31 quarters, the total value is 31 x $0.25 = $7.75. If we have 31 dimes, the total is $3.10. Clearly most of our coins will be dimes, with only a few quarters. What if we have 30 dimes and 1 quarter? Then our total is $3.00 + $0.25 = $3.25. We are closer. Let's try 29 dimes and 2 quarters: $2.90 + $0.50 = $3.40. Closer still. What about 25 dimes and 6 quarters? $2.50 + $1.50 = $4.00. Now we know that 25 of the coins are dimes and 6 are quarters. However, that's not the final answer. We need to show what probability there is of dropping a dime. To do this, we get the percentage of dimes in the total: 25 dimes divided by 31 coins total, or 80.6%.

81. **The answer is C.** Since there are five possible answer choices, we can try testing each answer choice against the rules in the problem. We know that if we make groups of three (this is just like dividing by three), there are no remainders. Immediately we can eliminate some answer choices: A, B, and D are not divisible by three with no remainder. Now, let's try making groups of four or dividing by four: 27 divided by 4 is 6, with three left over. 28 divided by 4 is 7, with nothing left over. Only choice C fits all rules.

82. **The answer is E.** Think about what this problem means in a visual way – Mikey has a rectangle measuring 24 by 13, and he wants to make 4 x 4 squares.

We know that 6 of these squares could fit along the 24 inch side, because 6 x 4 = 24. On the 13 inch side, only 3 of the 4 inch squares will fit, because 3 x 4 = 12, and 4 x 4 = 16, which is too big to fit on the 13 inch cardboard.
We can make a total of 6 x 3 = 18 squares.

Student's Name: _____   Admissions ID Code: _____

Student's Signature: _____   Date of Birth: _____

PRACTICE TEST 3
FOR
HUNTER COLLEGE HIGH SCHOOL
EXAMINATION

(THIS TEST WAS CREATED BASED ON A SAMPLE TEST PROVIDED BY HUNTER COLLEGE HIGH SCHOOL)

This test contains three sections: 48 multiple-choice **English Language Arts questions**, **a Writing Assignment**, and 35 multiple-choice **Mathematics questions**.

Each multiple-choice question is followed by **five possible answers: A, B, C, D, or E.** Choose the best answer for each question. You may make marks in this test booklet; use the space between questions and the blank pages in your booklet for scrap paper. **There is no penalty for guessing.**

On the answer sheet, carefully blacken the circle that contains the letter of the answer you select. Use only a Number 2 pencil for the multiple-choice sections. If you wish to change an answer, carefully erase the wrong answer completely and mark your new answer. **As soon as you finish one section of the test, go on to the next section. Monitor the time the proctor writes on the board.**

Calculators are not permitted.

You have a total of **three hours to complete the examination**, including the Writing Assignment.

If you complete the test before the time is up, review your previous work to correct for errors. Make sure that your answer sheet is accurately and cleanly prepared.

You may not remove any page from this booklet or take papers from the test room.

Kweller Prep

LANGUAGE ARTS
Critical Reading

Each of the following passages is followed by questions based on its content. Choose the letter of the answer that best reflects what is stated or implied by the passage.

Reading Passage A

This passage was adapted from "The Necklace," by Guy de Maupassant.

1   She was one of those pretty, charming women who are born, as if by an error of Fate, into a petty official's family. She had no dowry, no hopes, nor the slightest chance of being loved and married by a rich man—so she slipped into marriage with a minor civil servant.

5   Unable to afford jewels, she dressed simply: But she was wretched, for women have neither caste nor breeding—in them beauty, grace, and charm replace pride of birth. Innate refinement, instinctive elegance, and wit give them their place on the only scale that counts, and these make humble girls the peers of the grandest ladies.

She suffered, feeling that every luxury should rightly have been hers. The
10   poverty of her rooms—the shabby walls, the worn furniture, the ugly upholstery caused her pain. All these things that another woman of her class would not even have noticed, made her angry. The very sight of the little Breton girl who cleaned for her awoke rueful thoughts and the wildest dreams in her mind. She dreamt of rooms with Oriental hangings, lighted by tall, bronze torches, and with two huge
15   footmen in knee breeches made drowsy by the heat from the stove, asleep in the wide armchairs. She dreamt of great drawing rooms upholstered in old silks, with fragile little tables holding priceless knickknacks, and of enchanting little sitting rooms designed for tea-time chats with famous, sought-after men whose attentions all women longed for.

20   She sat down to dinner at her round table with its three-day-old cloth, and watched her husband lift the lid of the soup tureen and delightedly exclaim: "Ah, a good homemade beef stew! There's nothing better!" She visualized elegant dinners with gleaming silver and gorgeous china. She yearned for wall hangings peopled with knights and ladies and exotic birds in a fairy forest. She dreamt of eating the pink
25   flesh of trout or the wings of grouse. She had no proper wardrobe, no jewels, nothing. And those were the only things that she loved—she felt she was made for them. She would have so loved to charm, to be envied, to be admired and sought after.

She had a rich friend, an old school friend whom she refused to visit, because she suffered so keenly when she returned home. She would weep whole days, with
30   grief, regret, despair, and misery.

1. Which word best describes the actual living conditions of the couple?
   (A) destitute
   (B) poor
   (C) comfortable
   (D) wealthy
   (E) constantly changing

2. Regarding her marriage, the woman in this passage,
   (A) married but was ashamed of her husband's insignificant position.
   (B) married on the rebound after a wealthy suitor abandoned her.
   (C) married for love without realizing the consequences to her social standing.
   (D) never loved her husband.
   (E) married to make someone jealous.

3. In this passage, it is clear that the husband's values are different from his wife's in that he
   (A) enjoys simple comforts of his home.
   (B) wants even more than she does.
   (C) does morally questionable things.
   (D) expects his wife to be his servant.
   (E) will not provide for his wife.

4. The woman in this passage can best be described as
   (A) peaceful
   (B) pensive
   (C) sulky
   (D) manic
   (E) cheerful

5. The main purpose of the passage is
   (A) to have the reader feel great sympathy for the wife.
   (B) to have the reader feel great sympathy for the husband.
   (C) to show the class distinctions that were obvious during the setting
   (D) to show the reader how selfish and self-centered the wife is
   (E) to provide the reader with historical information

6. Maupassant uses words like "shabby," "worn," and "ugly" to describe how the wife perceives her home. These words are what part of speech?
   (A) adjectives
   (B) adverbs
   (C) nouns
   (D) verbs
   (E) prepositions

7. The passage implies that the woman does not contact her old friend because she
   (A) is afraid her friend will have changed.
   (B) envies the woman's wealth.
   (C) does not know how to contact her.
   (D) does not like the woman's home.
   (E) is in love with the woman's husband.

8. According to this passage, the woman dreams of
   (A) love
   (B) material wealth
   (C) fate
   (D) friendship
   (E) travel

9. The narrator's point of view is one of:
   (A) a friend of the woman
   (B) the husband
   (C) an all-knowing observer
   (D) the woman
   (E) an unknown relative of the woman

10. In line 27, the woman feels that wealth would
    (A) make her marriage happier
    (B) her to weep
    (C) make her charming and envied
    (D) provide an escape for her
    (E) allow her to be ignored

Reading Passage B
The following passage describes the composition and nature of ivory.

Ivory skin, ivory teeth, Ivory Soap, Ivory Snow—we hear "ivory" used all the time to describe something fair, white, and pure. But where does ivory come from, and what exactly is it? Is it natural or man-made? Is it a modifier, meaning something pure and white, or is it a specialized and discrete substance?

Historically, the word *ivory* has been applied to the tusks of elephants. However, the chemical structure of the teeth and tusks of mammals is the same regardless of the species of origin, and the trade in certain teeth and tusks other than elephant is well established and widespread. Therefore, ivory can correctly be used to describe any mammalian tooth or tusk of commercial interest that is large enough to be carved or scrimshawed. Teeth and tusks have the same origins. Teeth are specialized structures adapted for food mastication. Tusks, which are extremely large teeth projecting beyond the lips, have evolved from teeth and give certain species an evolutionary advantage that goes beyond chewing and breaking down food in digestible pieces. Furthermore, the tusk can be used to actually secure food through hunting, killing, and then breaking up large chunks of food into manageable bits.

The teeth of most mammals consist of a root as well as the tusk proper. Teeth and tusks have the same physical structures: pulp cavity, dentine, cementum, and enamel. The innermost area is the pulp cavity. The pulp cavity is an empty space within the tooth that conforms to the shape of the pulp. Odontoblastic cells line the pulp cavity and are responsible for the production of dentine. Dentine, which is the main component of carved ivory objects, forms a layer of consistent thickness around the pulp cavity and comprises the bulk of the tooth and tusk. Dentine is a mineralized connective tissue with an organic matrix of collagenous proteins. The inorganic component of dentine consists of dahllite. Dentine contains a microscopic structure called dentinal tubules which are micro-canals that radiate outward through the dentine from the pulp cavity to the exterior cementum border.

These canals have different configurations in different ivories and their diameter ranges between 0.8 and 2.2 microns. Their length is dictated by the radius of the tusk. The three dimensional configuration of the dentinal tubules is under genetic control and is therefore a characteristic unique to the order of the mammal.

Exterior to the dentine lies the cementum layer. Cementum forms a layer surrounding the dentine of tooth and tusk roots. Its main function is to adhere the tooth and tusk root to the mandibular and maxillary jaw bones. Incremental lines are commonly seen in cementum.

Enamel, the hardest animal tissue, covers the surface of the tooth or tusk which receives the most wear, such as the tip or crown. Ameloblasts are responsible for the formation of enamel and are lost after the enamel process is complete. Enamel exhibits a prismatic structure with prisms that run perpendicular to the crown or tip. Enamel prism patterns can have both taxonomic and evolutionary significance.

Tooth and tusk ivory can be carved into an almost infinite variety of shapes and objects. Examples of carved ivory objects are netsukes, jewelry, flatware handles, furniture inlays, and piano keys. Additionally, wart hog tusks, and teeth from sperm whales, killer whales, and hippos can also be scrimshawed or superficially carved, thus retaining their original shapes as morphologically recognizable objects. The identification of ivory and ivory substitutes is based on the physical and chemical class characteristics of these materials. A common approach to identification is to use the macroscopic and microscopic physical characteristics of ivory in combination with a simple chemical test using ultraviolet light.

11. In line 4, "discrete" means
    (A) sensitive
    (B) distinct
    (C) careful
    (D) precise
    (E) collective

12. Which of the following titles is most appropriate for this passage?
    (A) Ivory: An Endangered Species
    (B) Elephants, Ivory, and Widespread Hunting in Africa
    (C) Ivory: Is it Organic or Inorganic
    (D) Uncovering the Truth About Natural Ivory
    (E) A Brief History of Ivory

13. The word "scrimshawed" in line 41 most likely means
    (A) floated
    (B) waxed
    (C) carved
    (D) sunk
    (E) recycled

14. Which of the following is NOT part of the physical structure of the teeth as described in the third paragraph?
    (A) pulp cavity
    (B) dentine
    (C) cementum
    (D) tusk
    (E) enamel

15. As used in line 10, "mastication" means
    (A) digestion
    (B) tasting
    (C) biting
    (D) chewing
    (E) swallowing

16. Dentine tubules
    (A) are a layer surrounding the tooth and tusk roots.
    (B) are micro-canals that radiate outward through the dentine.
    (C) cover the surface of the tooth or tusk.
    (D) are extremely large teeth projecting beyond the lips.
    (E) are located on the roof of the mouth

17. According to the article, which of the following is an inorganic substance?
    (A) cementum
    (B) dentine
    (C) dahllite
    (D) emeloblasts
    (E) cells

18. In line 39, "netsukes" are
    (A) honed sharks teeth
    (B) small statues
    (C) a group of people
    (D) piano keys
    (E) another name for ivory

19. According to the passage, how can natural ivory be authenticated?
    (A) by ultraviolet light
    (B) by gamma rays
    (C) by physical observation
    (D) by osmosis
    (E) by radiation

20. According to this article, the term "ivory" can be used to describe
    (A) any tooth of any animal
    (B) any mammalian tooth that is large enough to be carved
    (C) the teeth of humans
    (D) the bones of any mammal
    (E) the bones of any animal

Reading Passage C
In the following passage, the author tells of public art and its functions.

In Manhattan's Eighth Avenue/Fourteenth Street subway station, a grinning bronze alligator with human hands pops out of a manhole cover to grab a bronze "baby" whose head is the shape of a moneybag. In the Bronx General Post Office, a giant 13-panel painting called *Resources of America* celebrates the hard work and industrialism of America in the first half of the twentieth century. And in Brooklyn's MetroTech Center, just over the Brooklyn Bridge, several installations of art are on view at any given time—from an iron lasso resembling a giant charm bracelet to a series of wagons that play recordings of great American poems to a life-sized seeing eye dog that looks so real people are constantly stopping to pet it.

There exists in every city a symbiotic relationship between the city and its art. When we hear the term *art*, we tend to think of private art—the kind displayed in private spaces such as museums, concert halls, and galleries. But there is a growing interest in, and respect for, public art: the kind of art created for and displayed in public spaces such as parks, building lobbies, and sidewalks.

Although all art is inherently public—created in order to convey an idea or emotion to others—"public art," as opposed to art that is sequestered in museums and galleries, is art specifically designed for a public arena where the art will be encountered by people in their normal day-to-day activities. Public art can be purely ornamental or highly functional; it can be as subtle as a decorative door knob or as conspicuous as the Chicago Picasso. It is also an essential element of effective urban design.

The more obvious forms of public art include monuments, sculptures, fountains, murals, and gardens. But public art also takes the form of ornamental benches or street lights, decorative manhole covers, and mosaics on trash bins. Many city dwellers would be surprised to discover just how much public art is really around them and how much art they have passed by without noticing, and how much impact public art has on their day-to-day lives.

Public art fulfills several functions essential to the health of a city and its citizens. It educates about history and culture—of the artist, the neighborhood, the city, the nation. Public art is also a "place-making device" that instantly creates memorable, experiential landmarks, fashioning a unique identity for a public place, personalizing it and giving it a specific character. It stimulates the public, challenging viewers to interpret the art and arousing their emotions, and it promotes community by stimulating interaction among viewers. In serving these multiple and important functions, public art beautifies the area and regenerates both the place and the viewer.

One question often debated in public art forums is whether public art should be created *with* or *by* the public rather than *for* the public. Increasingly, cities and artists are recognizing the importance of creating works with meaning for the intended audience, and this generally requires direct input from the community or from an artist entrenched in that community. At the same time, however, art created for the community by an "outsider" often adds fresh perspective. Thus, cities and their citizens are best served by a combination of public art created *by* members of the community, art created with input *from* members of the community, and art created by others *for* the community.

21. According to line 12, public art is displayed in places such as
    (A) people's homes
    (B) religious buildings
    (C) government buildings
    (D) parks and sidewalks
    (E) university campuses

22. The word "inherently" in line 15 means
    (A) unimportant
    (B) essential
    (C) meaningless
    (D) overlooked
    (E) characteristic

23. In the first paragraph of this passage, the author
    (A) describes one particular piece of art.
    (B) summarizes the importance of art in society.
    (C) tries to define exactly what art is.
    (D) names several prominent artists.
    (E) describes different examples of public art.

24. Which of the following is not a form that public art might take, as described in the fourth paragraph?
    (A) monuments
    (B) sculptures
    (C) fountains
    (D) gardens
    (E) buildings

25. Which of the following is NOT one of the functions of public art mentioned in the fifth paragraph?
    (A) educates the public about history and culture.
    (B) creates memorable landmarks.
    (C) stimulates the economy.
    (D) stimulates the public.
    (E) beautifies the area.

26. What is the best definition of the word "ornamental" as it appears in line 19?
    (A) popular
    (B) flashy
    (C) functional
    (D) decorative
    (E) mysterious

27. According to the last paragraph of this article, what question about public art has recently been debated?
    (A) Should art be created with the public rather than for the public?
    (B) What should artists be paid?
    (C) Should art be functional?
    (D) Should art be modern or traditional?
    (E) Should art incorporate different cultures?

28. According to the last paragraph, what is a benefit of having an "outsider" create public art?
    (A) It adds life to the community.
    (B) It sparks debate.
    (C) It gives people something to think about.
    (D) It creates a fresh perspective.
    (E) It adds diversity to the community.

29. In line 20, "conspicuous" most likely means
    (A) bright
    (B) subtle
    (C) attracting attention
    (D) intelligent
    (E) bringing controversy

30. According to the fifth paragraph, art can give a place a unique identity by
    (A) surprising its viewers.
    (B) stimulating interaction among the viewers.
    (C) giving the place a new function.
    (D) giving it a specific character.
    (E) bringing bright colors to an otherwise dull place.

31. In line 16, the word "sequestered" most likely means
    (A) out in the open
    (B) disposed of
    (C) unknown
    (D) hidden away
    (E) famous

Reading Passage D

The following selection explains the origins of sushi, and its popularity in the United States.

1   Burgers, fries, pizza, raw fish. Raw fish? Fast food in America is changing. *Sushi*, the thousand year old Japanese delicacy, was once thought of in this country as unpalatable and too exotic. But tastes have changed, for a number of reasons. Beginning in the 1970s, Americans became increasingly more aware of diet and
5   health issues, and began rejecting their traditional red-meat diets in favor of healthier, lowerfat choices such as fish, poultry, whole grains, rice, and vegetables. The way food was prepared began to change, too; rather than frying food, people started opting for broiled, steamed, and raw versions. *Sushi*, a combination of rice and fish, fit the bill. In addition, that same decade saw Japan become an important global
10 economic force, and companies began flocking to the country to do business. All things Japanese, including décor, clothing, and cuisine, became popular.

    Sushi started small in the United States, in a handful of restaurants in big cities. But it caught on. Today, *sushi* consumption in American restaurants is 40% greater than it was in the late 1990s, according to the National Restaurant Association.
15 The concession stands at almost every major league stadium sell *sushi*, and many colleges and universities offer it in their dining halls. But we're not just eating it out. The National Sushi Association reports that there are over 5,000 *sushi* bars in supermarkets, and that number is growing monthly. This incredible growth in availability and consumption points to the fact that Americans have decided that
20 *sushi* isn't just good for them, or just convenient, but that this once-scorned food is truly delicious.

    The origins of this food trend may be found in Asia, where it was developed as a way of preserving fish. Fresh, cleaned fish was pressed between rice and salt and weighted with a heavy stone over a period of several months. During this time, the
25 rice fermented, producing lactic acid that pickled and preserved the fish. For many years, the fish was eaten and the rice was discarded. But about 500 years ago, that changed, and *hako-zushi* (boxed *sushi*) was created. In this type of *sushi*, the rice and fish are pressed together in a box, and are consumed together.

    In 1824, Yohei Hanaya of Edo (now called Tokyo) eliminated the fermenta-
30 tion process, and began serving fresh slices of seafood on bases of vinegared rice. The vinegar was probably used to mimic the taste of fermented *sushi*. In fact, the word *sushi* actually refers to any vinegared rice dish, and not to the fish, as many Americans believe (the fish is called *sashimi*). In Japanese, when *sushi* is combined with a modifier, it changes to the word *zushi*.

35 Chef Yohei's invention, called *nigiri zushi*, is still served today. It now refers to a slice of fish (cooked or uncooked) that is pressed by hand onto a serving of rice. Popular choices include *ama ebi* (raw shrimp), *shime saba* (marinated mackerel), and *maguro* (tuna). In addition to the vinegar flavor in the rice, *nigiri zushi* typically contains a taste of horseradish (*wasabi*), and is served with soy sauce for dipping.

40 *Maki zushi* contains strips of fish or vegetables rolled in rice and wrapped in thin sheets of *nori*, or dried seaweed. Popular ingredients include smoked salmon, fresh crab, shrimp, octopus, raw clams, and sea urchin. Americans have invented many of their own *maki zushi* combinations, including the California roll, which contains imitation crabmeat and avocado. They have also made innovations in the
45 construction of *maki zushi*. Some American *sushi* bars switch the placement of *nori* and rice, while others don't use *nori*, and instead roll the *maki zushi* in fish roe. These colorful, crunchy eggs add to the visual and taste appeal of the dish.

32. What change occurred in the 1970s that caused sushi to become more popular?
    (A) People began to travel more.
    (B) It became fashionable to eat as sushi bars.
    (C) It became trendy to try new foods.
    (D) People began watching Japanese television.
    (E) People became more health conscious.

33. According to this passage, what other food also gained popularity in the 1970s?
    (A) whole grains
    (B) pepperoni pizza
    (C) fried chicken
    (D) fast-food burgers
    (E) fried rice

34. What was Yohei Hanay's contribution to *sushi*?
    (A) he pressed the fish and rice tighter in a box.
    (B) he introduced the population of Edo to the dish.
    (C) He smoked the fish before putting it on vinegared rice.
    (D) He used wasabi to flavor it.
    (E) He used raw fish

35. In this passage, *shime* most likely means
    (A) salmon
    (B) shrimp
    (C) marinated
    (D) roe
    (E) seaweed

36. All of the following can be explicitly answered by reading this passage except
    (A) what is the definition of the word sushi?
    (B) did Japan's economic status have a bearing on sushi's popularity?
    (C) have Americans adapted sushi to make it more in keeping with their tastes?
    (D) why do some Americans prefer maki zushi over nigiri zushi?
    (E) what happens to fish when it is layered with rice and left for a period of months?

37. The passage describes Americans *sushi* consumption as
    (A) higher than it was several years ago
    (B) important when watching sports
    (C) most often eaten as take-out
    (D) a trend due to supermarket marketing
    (E) beginning for many in college

38. In line 3, the word "unpalatable" means
    (A) not visually appealing
    (B) tastes bad
    (C) smells bad
    (D) too expensive
    (E) rough to touch

39. According to this article, the difference between *sushi* and *zushi* is that
    (A) they are two different kinds of fish
    (B) one includes rice and one does not
    (C) one is used on its own and one has modifiers
    (D) one is the American spelling, one is the Japanese spelling
    (E) one has soy cause and one does not

40. In the third paragraph, the author discusses that when fish is pickled
    (A) it becomes crisp.
    (B) it turns green.
    (C) it dissolves into the rice.
    (D) it is preserved
    (E) it dries out.

41. Which of the following is not true about sushi's popularity?
    (A) Sushi has become more popular than hamburgers.
    (B) Today, Americans eat 40% more sushi than in the late 1990s.
    (C) Concession stands at major league stadiums sells it.
    (D) Many colleges offer sushi in their dining halls.
    (E) There are over 5,000 sushi bars in supermarkets.

42. The word "delicacy" as used in line 2 can best be defined as
    (A) an choice or expensive food
    (B) a cultural experience
    (C) a profitable item
    (D) something popular
    (E) something most people don't know about

Reading Passage E

This passage is excerpted from "Leonardo da Vinci" from Knights of Art: Stories of the Italian Painters by Amy Steedman, 1907.

On the sunny slopes of Monte Albano, between Florence and Pisa, the little town of Vinci lay high among the rocks that crowned the steep hillside. Here in the year 1452 Leonardo, son of Ser Piero da Vinci, was born. It was in the age when people told fortunes by the stars, and when a baby was born they would eagerly look up and decide whether it was a lucky or unlucky star which shone upon the child. Surely if it had been possible in this way to tell what fortune awaited the little Leonardo, a strange new star must have shone that night, brighter than the others and unlike the rest in the dazzling light of its strength and beauty.

Leonardo was always a strange child. Even his beauty was not like that of other children. He had the most wonderful waving hair, falling in regular ripples, like the waters of a fountain, the color of bright gold, and soft as spun silk. His eyes were blue and clear, with a mysterious light in them, not the warm light of a sunny sky, but rather the blue that glints in the iceberg. They were merry eyes too, when he laughed, but underneath was always that strange cold look. There was a charm about his smile which no one could resist, and he was a favorite with all. Yet people shook their heads sometimes as they looked at him, and they talked in whispers of the old witch who had lent her goat to nourish the little Leonardo when he was a baby. The woman was a dealer in black magic, and who knew but that the child might be a changeling?

It was the old grandmother, Mona Lena, who brought Leonardo up and spoilt him not a little. His father, Ser Piero, was a lawyer, and spent most of his time in Florence, but when he returned to the old castle of Vinci, he began to give Leonardo lessons and tried to find out what the boy was fit for. But Leonardo hated those lessons and would not learn, so when he was seven years old he was sent to school.

This did not answer any better. The rough play of the boys was not to his liking. When he saw them drag the wings off butterflies, or torture any animal that fell into their hands, his face grew white with pain, and he would take no share in their games. The Latin grammar, too, was a terrible task, while the many things he longed to know no one taught him.

So it happened that many a time, instead of going to school, he would slip away and escape up into the hills, as happy as a little wild goat. Here was all the sweet fresh air of heaven, instead of the stuffy schoolroom. Here were no cruel, clumsy boys, but all the wild creatures that he loved. Here he could learn the real things his heart was hungry to know, not merely words which meant nothing and led to nowhere.

For hours he would lie perfectly still with his heels in the air and his chin resting in his hands, as he watched a spider weaving its web, breathless with interest to see how the delicate threads were turned in and out. The gaily painted butterflies, the fat buzzing bees, the little sharp-tongued green lizards, he loved to watch them all, but above everything he loved the birds. Oh, if only he too had wings to dart like the swallows, and swoop and sail and dart again! What was the secret power in their wings? Surely by watching he might learn it. Sometimes it seemed as if his heart would burst with the longing to learn that secret. It was always the hidden reason of things that he desired to know. Much as he loved the flowers he must pull their petals off, one by one, to see how each was joined, to wonder at the dusty pollen, and touch the honey-covered stamens. Then when the sun began to sink he would turn sadly homewards, very hungry, with torn clothes and tired feet, but with a store of sunshine in his heart.

His grandmother shook her head when Leonardo appeared after one of his days of wandering.

"I know thou shouldst be whipped for playing truant," she said;" and I should also punish thee for tearing thy clothes."

"Ah! But thou wilt not whip me," answered Leonardo, smiling at her with his curious quiet smile, for he had full confidence in her love.

"Well, I love to see thee happy, and I will not punish thee this time," said his grandmother; "but if these tales reach thy father's ears, he will not be so tender as I am towards thee."

And, sure enough, the very next time that a complaint was made from the school, his father happened to be at home, and then the storm burst.

"Next time I will flog thee," said Ser Piero sternly, with rising anger at the careless air of the boy. "Meanwhile we will see what a little imprisonment will do towards making thee a better child."

Then he took the boy by the shoulders and led him to a little dark cupboard under the stairs, and there shut him up for three whole days.

There was no kicking or beating at the locked door. Leonardo sat quietly there in the dark, thinking his own thoughts, and wondering why there seemed so little justice in the world. But soon even that wonder passed away, and as usual when he was alone he began to dream dreams of the time when he should have learned the swallows' secrets and should have wings like theirs.

But if there were complaints about Leonardo's dislike of the boys and the Latin grammar, there would be none about the lessons he chose to learn. Indeed, some of the masters began to dread the boy's eager questions, which were sometimes more than they could answer. Scarcely had he begun the study of arithmetic than he made such rapid progress, and wanted to puzzle out so many problems, that the masters were amazed. His mind seemed always eagerly asking for more light, and was never satisfied.

43. What can you infer about Leonardo's teachers from the last paragraph of the passage?
    (A) They were afraid he would ask questions they could not answer.
    (B) They thought he was unable to learn.
    (C) They thought he had no desire to learn.
    (D) They believed he should try to get along with the other students.

44. The person or people who were most responsible for raising Leonardo were his:
    (A) father.
    (B) mother.
    (C) teachers.
    (D) grandmother.

45. It can be inferred from the passage that Leonardo:
    I. did not mind being alone.
    II. was fascinated by flight.
    III. was popular with the other students.
    (A) I and II only
    (B) I, II, and III
    (C) I only
    (D) II only

46. What year was Leonardo first sent to school?
    (A) 1452
    (B) 1455
    (C) 1459
    (D) 1461

47. According to the passage, all the following are true EXCEPT:
    (A) Leonardo enjoyed learning Latin grammar.
    (B) Leonardo enjoyed learning math.
    (C) Leonardo enjoyed studying nature.
    (D) Leonardo was curious about the way things worked.

48. Which of the following statements best sums up what is meant by lines 43–45 ("Much as he loved the flowers he must pull their petals off, one by one, to see how each was joined, to wonder at the dusty pollen, and touch the honey-covered stamens")?
    (A) Leonardo's desire to learn how things worked was stronger than his affection for nature.
    (B) Leonardo's love of flowers drove him to destroy them.
    (C) Leonardo revered all of nature.
    (D) Leonardo's curiosity led him to destructive acts.

Writing Assignment

New York City is a city of contrasts and opposites. Multimillion-dollar luxury apartments next door to housing projects. The traffic-clogged grid of blocks and avenues interrupted by the green space expanse of Central Park. Fourth-generation New Yorkers living and working alongside new immigrants.

Write an essay about two features of New York that you are familiar with. This can be two kinds of people, two physical features, two aspects of daily life. Explore the way in which these two features of New York that you are familiar with can be compared and contrasted.

Your task is to write an essay that compares the similarities and differences between these two features. Use your experience with them to provide specific details about each feature. Describe what makes each object, person, location, etc. unique, explain what makes these two things both similar and different from each other.

You must write an essay in which you:

- Identify features of New York that you are familiar with
- Provide descriptions of what makes each object, person, place, etc. unique
- Identify the similarities and differences between these two features
- Explain what these features represent to you about living in New York

MATHEMATICS

49. If *A* and *B* are whole numbers between 0 and 9 (both included), find A – B so that
3.2857 + 15.9AB9 = 19.2636

(A) 7   (B) 0   (C) 3   (D) 1   (E) 6

50. If the distance between the numbers 4.2 and -1.68 on the number line is multiplied by 0.24 the result is:

(A) 1.4112   (B) 0.6048   (C) 1.4212   (D) 1.5112   (E) –0.6048

51. What is the value of $\dfrac{3}{5} \div \left(\dfrac{3}{2}\right)^2 \div \dfrac{1}{4}$?

(A) $\dfrac{1}{10}$ (B) $\dfrac{27}{5}$ (C) $\dfrac{1}{15}$ (D) $\dfrac{8}{5}$ (E) $\dfrac{16}{15}$

52. Write the expression $\dfrac{2}{5} \div \dfrac{6}{25} \times \dfrac{4}{9}$ in its lowest terms

(A) $\dfrac{20}{9}$ (B) $\dfrac{10}{27}$ (C) $\dfrac{20}{27}$ (D) $\dfrac{48}{375}$ (E) $\dfrac{9}{75}$

53. What is the value of the following expression?

$$\dfrac{\dfrac{11}{3} \div \dfrac{1}{4}}{\dfrac{5}{6} - \dfrac{7}{3} + 1}$$

(A) $-\dfrac{44}{3}$ (B) $-\dfrac{88}{3}$ (C) $\dfrac{22}{3}$ (D) $-\dfrac{22}{12}$ (E) $\dfrac{22}{12}$

54. You are given the pattern 1357911131517..... What is the position in the pattern of the first 8 that we find that is preceded by a 1?

   (A) 216th   (B) 218th   (C) 77th   (D) 78th   (E) 217th

55. A car parking station charges $6 fixed amount for the first 1.5 hours and $1.50 per additional half hour. How much money in dollars will Sarah pay if she parks her car in the station at 6pm and leaves at 11pm?

   (A) 10.5   (B) 16.5   (C) 18   (D) 15   (E) 19.5

56. The average score of John's first four math tests is 79% and his average score in the next two math tests is 85%. Which of the following represents John's average score in all six math tests?

   (A) 82%   (B) 81%   (C) 85%   (D) 82.5%   (E) 81.5%

57. Peter and Julia are siblings and hold separate bank accounts. Their current balance is $3250 and $1720 respectively. Starting tomorrow, Peter will take $10 from his account every day, while Julia will add $20 to her account every day. After how many days will the two accounts have the same balance?

   (A) 51   (B) 30   (C) 50   (D) 166   (E) 153

58. Suzan, Tim, Greg, Annie and Mat are all children with different ages. If they were to be placed in a line according to their age, Suzan would get the middle position and Greg would stand right next to her. Moreover Mat is younger than Greg and Tim is younger than Annie. Which of the following statements is true?

   (A) The youngest person must be Mat.
   (B) Tim cannot be placed in the leftmost or rightmost position.
   (C) The oldest person must be Annie.
   (D) Both Mat and Tim are younger than Suzan.
   (E) Annie is the oldest person only if Greg is older than Suzan.

Mathematics

59. The radius of the circle in the below figure is 5 inches and O is its center. The radius of the semicircle included in the circle is 4 inches and F is its center. EF equals to 8 inches. What is the length of GO segment in inches?

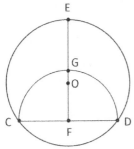

(A) 1   (B) $\frac{1}{2}$ (C) $\frac{1}{8}$ (D) 2   (E) 1.5

60. When the 34th number of the pattern 1, 4, 7, 10, 13, 16, 19,…is subtracted from the 49th odd natural number, what is the result? (The natural numbers are 1, 2, 3, 4,…)

(A) -2   (B) 3   (C) 15   (D) 14   (E) -3

61. For the 17th even natural number what is the number of ways it can be written as the sum of two different prime numbers? (A prime number is a number that has only two factors, 1 and itself; 1 is not a prime number. The natural numbers are 1, 2, 3, 4,…)

(A) 4   (B) 2   (C) 0   (D) 1   (E) 3

62. There are six people in a room sitting at a round table. Each person has already shaken hands with the two persons sitting next to them exactly once. How many more unique handshakes need to happen so that all people have shaken hands with each other exactly once?

(A) 9   (B) 15   (C) 10   (D) 14   (E) 21

63. In this grid, the dots are spaced one unit apart, horizontally and vertically. What is the number of square units of the shaded area?

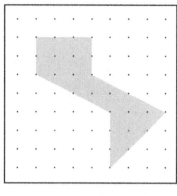

(A) 12   (B) 16   (C) 14   (D) 10.5   (E) 16.5

64. In the expression below, each letter represents a one-digit number. Where the same letter appears, it represents the same number in each case. Each distinct letter represents a different number. In order to make the equation true, what number must replace B ?

$$\begin{array}{r} AAA \\ \times\ AB \\ \hline 20{,}868 \end{array}$$

(A) 4   (B) 5   (C) 7   (D) 3   (E) 9

65. If someone opens an account in a bank and puts $100 for 1 year, at the end of the year his amount will be increased by 4% ($4 in this case). Mark opens this type of account and makes an initial deposit of $500. What percent (to the nearest tenth) of this $500 is the total interest paid into the account after 3 years.

(A) 12   (B) 12.5   (C) 12.8   (D) 13   (E) 14

66. Mike wants to order pizza for his friends. There are 3 different sizes (medium, large, extra), 3 different types of crust (thin, classic, italian) and 4 sets of toppings (margherita, capricioza, peperoni, vegie). How many different ways does Mike have to order one pizza?

(A) 3   (B) 28   (C) 9   (D) 36   (E) 16

Mathematics

67. John sold his piano to Peter for 25% more than he paid for it. After a few months Peter sold the piano to Emma for 13% less than he paid for it. What percent of the original price did Emma pay for the piano?
(A) 88% (B) 109% (C) 112% (D) 90% (E) 92%

68. Mary wants to buy candies with an amount of money she has in her pocket. We know that if she had $3.20 more money she could buy 120 candies while if she had $2.40 less money she could buy 85 candies. What is the price per candy?
(A) $1.6 (B) 18¢ (C) 16¢ (D) 6.25¢ (E) $8

69. How many 4 – sided figures are in this diagram?

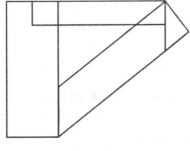

(A) 12 (B) 9 (C) 8 (D) 11 (E) 10

70. A swimming pool in a luxury hotel measures 15 meters length and 7 meters width, and when it is filled the depth of the water is 1.8 meters. The hotel owner wants to construct a kids' pool of 6 meters length and 5 meters width. What should be the depth of the water in meters in the kids' pool, so that its volume will be 10% of the volume of the water in the big pool when filled?
(A) 0.063 (B) 0.189 (C) 1.89 (D) 0.63 (E) 0.06

71. In a photocopy center 2,070 pages need to be copied. Photocopy machine A is twice as fast as another photocopy machine B and when working together they can complete this job in half an hour. The two machines start copying and after 10 minutes a third photocopy machine C, which is as fast as A, is added in the work to speed up the process. How many minutes earlier will the job finish?
(A) 9 (B) 12 (C) 10 (D) 8 (E) 7

72. The following diagram depicts the routes that George and Harry walked starting from point A. George moved from A to B and then headed towards C while Harry took the different direction at point B and moved towards point D. If all angles shown in the figure are right angles and the numbers shown represent hundred meters, what is the total distance in meters that both George and Harry walked?

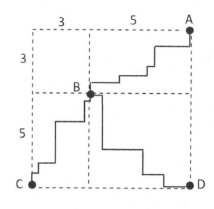

(A) 2,200 (B) 1,100 (C) 1,300 (D) 3,400 (E) 2,100

73. Name the three digit number ABC that satisfies all of the following conditions:
   i) A, B, C can be any of the numbers 2, 5, 6 and 7 each used once
   ii) BC forms a two digit number divisible by 6
   iii) ABC forms a three digit number divisible by 3

(A) 576 (B) 762 (C) 672 (D) 675 (E) 526

74. The people of a small town are called to vote for mayor's consultants. There are 4 candidates A, B, C and D and each citizen can vote for 2 or 3 candidates. If half of voters voted for 2 candidates and the other half for 3, and the candidates A, B, C and D got 243, 191, 186, and 160 votes respectively, how many voted?

(A) 312 (B) 156 (C) 195 (D) 390 (E) 308

Mathematics

75. A baker made the below box from cardboard and put inside fifteen round muffins, each with a radius of 1 inch. If the baker wants to have the muffins separated by liners, what is the total length of liners he will need to craft the appropriate grid and put it inside the box?

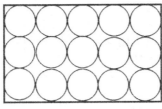

(A) 22" (B) 44" (C) 60" (D) 54" (E) 50"

76. Two trains are moving along straight lines towards each other. Both trains are traveling at constant but different speeds. The slower train is traveling at 90 miles per hour. 25 minutes before they meet their distance is 87.5 miles. What is the speed of the faster train in miles per hour?

(A) 100 (B) 120 (C) 125 (D) 135 (E) 140

77. You have a 6 x 6 x 6 inch cube that is made up of little 1 x 1 x 1 inch cubes. Someone tells you that some of the non-visible little cubes inside the cube might be miss-ing, but you cannot check as the cube is stuck on the ground. If indeed some of the little cubes are not there, what is the biggest possible number of them that could be missing?

(A) 216 (B) 64 (C) 96 (D) 124 (E) 80

78. If a 2-digit whole number is increased by 36 when its digits are reversed, what is the outcome of its first digit minus its second digit?

(A) 2 (B) -3 (C) -4 (D) 4 (E) 3

79. A bacterial population is growing rapidly and new bacteria are added every day. Each day, $\frac{3}{4}$ of the number of bacteria are new. How many times does the population increase in 2 days?

(A) 4 (B) 2 (C) 8 (D) 16 (E) 12

80. How many two digit numbers less than 66 are divisible by either 5 or 6?

(A) 17 (B) 21 (C) 19 (D) 20 (E) 22

81. Sandy has only pennies and nickels in her pocket. The pennies are 1 more than the nickels. Which of the following cannot be an amount that Sandy has?

(A) 43¢ (B) 37¢ (C) 59¢ (D) 25¢ (E) 67¢

82. How many 2-digit numbers satisfy all of the following conditions?
  i) When divided by 4 the remainder is 2
  ii) When divided by 5 the remainder is 3
  iii) When divided by 3 the remainder is 1

(A) 4 (B) 3 (C) 5 (D) 0 (E) 1

83. Paul is given a circular piece of paper with 5 inches radius and with the lengths of some segments written on. If all angles shown are right angles, what is the maximum number of 3-inch by 1-inch rectangles that he can cut from this piece of paper?

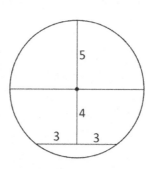

(A) 8 (B) 20 (C) 16 (D) 18 (E) 22

You have reached the end of the Mathematics section.
You may return to any part of the test to review your work.

ANSWER EXPLANATIONS FOR PRACTICE TEST 3

ENGLISH LANGUAGE ARTS

1. **Choice C is correct.** The husband had a civil servant's job and received a steady salary, the wife had a servant who cleaned for her, and the couple lived in a dwelling that had several rooms. This all implies that they lived comfortably.

2. **Choice A is correct.** The wife's thoughts in the first paragraph indicate that she wishes she had married a rich man. Instead she "slipped into marriage with a minor civil servant."

3. **Choice A is correct.** It is clear in this passage the husband enjoys the simple things in life. The narrator describes an evening when the husband and his wife sat down to a dinner of simple stew. The husband exclaimed, "what a good homemade beef stew! There is nothing better!" Meanwhile, his wife dreams of elegant china and silverware. This shows their different values.

4. **Choice C is correct.** The first paragraph includes the words "grief," "regret", "despair," and "misery," all of which suggest that the woman feels disappointed with her life.

5. **Choice D is correct.** This is reinforced at the end of the fourth paragraph; the wife admits she only loves rich things, believes she was made for them, and focuses all her desires on being "admired and sought after." She thinks only of herself at all times, even when it is clear to the reader that she has much to be thankful for.

6. **Choice A is correct.** Each of the words here describe a noun, so they are adjectives.

7. **Choice B is correct.** When the woman's friend is mentioned at the end of the passage, the reader can infer that the friend's wealth only makes her feel worse about her own perceived meager existence.

8. **Choice B is correct.** Throughout this entire passage, the woman is obsessed with material things. Even when she has much to be thankful for—a comfortable home, a pleasant husband—all she thinks about is how "poor" she is.

9. **Choice C is correct.** Though the narration closely follows the woman's thoughts, the story is told from a third person narrator who knows her thoughts and feelings.

10. **Choice C is the correct answer.** Line 27 says, specifically, "She would have so loved to charm, to be envied, to be admired and sought after."

11. **Choice B is correct.** "Discrete" means "distinct" and, as used in the passage, it is paired with "specialized," a context clue. Several of the other answer options are synonyms for its homophone "discreet," which means careful.

12. **Choice D is correct.** Choices A and C, while they do cover topics mentioned in the article, are too specific to be viable titles, while the topic in Choice E isn't really mentioned in the article. Choice D is broad-ranging enough to encompass the entire passage.

13. **Choice C is correct.** Scrimshawed means "carved." Because scrimshaw and enamel are wax-like substances, a less careful reader may choose Choice B, "waxed."

14. **Choice D is correct.** According to the passage, choices A, B, C, and D are all parts of the physical structure of teeth. Choice D, tusk, is not a component of teeth, but rather a type of tooth found in some mammals.

15. **Choice D is correct.** From the context of the lines in which "mastication" appears, it can be deduced that mastication means the act of chewing because tusks, evolved from teeth, are described as able to go beyond chewing.

16. **Choice B is correct.** According to the passage in line 23, dentine tubules "are micro-canals that radiate outward through the dentine from the pulp cavity to the exterior cementum border."

17. **Choice C is correct.** According to line 22, dahllite is an inorganic substance.

Answer Explanations For Practice Test 3

18. **Choice B is correct.** The text says, "examples of carved ivory objects are netsukes, jewelry, flatware handles, furniture inlays, and piano keys." We know from this sentence that a netsuke must be something carved from ivory. B is the only answer that would work.

19. **Choice A is correct.** Line 46 identifies how natural ivory can be authenticated using ultraviolet light.

20. **Choice B is correct.** According to the passage in line 8, ivory is defined as to "any mammalian tooth or tusk of commercial interest that is large enough to be carved or scrimshawed."

21. **Choice D is correct.** According to the article, public art is "the kind of art created for and displayed in public spaces such as parks, building lobbies, and sidewalks."

22. **Choice B is correct.** "Inherently" is an adverb that describes the essential nature of something. The context clue to answer this question is found in the same sentence: "all art is inherently public" because it is "created in order to convey an idea or emotion to others." The author is saying that an "essential" characteristic of art is that it is created for others.

23. **Choice E is correct.** In the very first paragraph, the author describes several pieces of art including a "grinning bronze alligator," "a 13-panel painting" and "a giant charm bracelet."

24. **Choice E is correct.** The article says that "the more obvious forms of public art include monuments, sculptures, fountains, murals and gardens." Buildings are not mentioned in this description.

25. **Choice C is correct.** The author lists numerous functions for artwork in the fifth paragraph, but stimulating the economy is not one of them.

26. **Choice D is correct.** The word "ornamental" means "decorative" in this context. The clue here is that the text says that art can be "ornamental or functional." We know then that something "ornamental" is the opposite of something is purely "functional," so decorative works as the definition.

27. **Choice A is correct.** In the last paragraph, the author discusses whether or not the community should be involved in the creation of public art.

28. **Choice D is correct.** In line 42, the author states, "art created for the community by an 'outsider' often adds fresh perspective."

29. **Choice C is correct.** The text states that art "can be as subtle as a decorative door knob or as conspicuous as the Chicago Picasso." The clue in this sentence is the word "subtle" which means sophisticated in a discreet sort of way. The structure of the sentence tells us that "subtle" will be the opposite of "conspicuous." So, while something subtle is complicated in a way you might not immediately notice, something conspicuous is immediately noticeable.

30. **Choice D is correct.** The paragraph states, specifically, that public art can fashion "a unique identity for a place, personalizing it and giving it a specific character."

31. **Choice D is correct.** The text mentions art that is "sequestered in museums and galleries," using it as a contrast for art that is public areas. Because we know that "sequestered" will be a contrast to something out in the open, we can conclude it means "hidden away."

32. **Choice E is correct.** The article mentions in the first paragraph how the United States became increasingly aware of concerns regarding eating healthy in the 1970s.

33. **Choice A is correct.** During the 1970s, Americans were beginning to eat healthier foods, such as vegetables, whole grains, fish, and poultry.

34. **Choice C is correct.** Paragraph 4 explains that he skipped the fermentation process, which means that the fish was fresh, or raw.

35. **Choice C is correct.** Paragraph 5 indicates that ama ebi is raw shrimp, and shime saba is marinated mackerel. You can infer that ebi means shrimp, because "raw" is not one of your choices. You can also infer that shime means marinated, because mackerel is not one of your choices. Therefore, shime ebi means marinated shrimp.

36. **Choice D is correct.** Nowhere in the passage does the author mention a preference for either type of sushi.

Answer Explanations For Practice Test 3

37. **Choice A is correct.** It is noted at the beginning of paragraph 2 that sushi consumption in America is 40% higher than it was in the late 1990s. The other answers might be true, they are not described in the passage.

38. **Choice B is correct.** "Unpalatable" may be defined as not agreeable to taste." You know the word "palate" as the roof of the mouth, so "unpalatable" most likely has to do with the sense of taste. The biggest clue to the definition comes when it is stated that Americans have decided, "this once-scorned food is truly delicious."

39. **Option C is correct** because the article describes in the fourth paragraph that zushi is when sushi is combined with a modifier.

40. **Choice D is correct.** The third paragraph describes how sushi was developed for the purpose of preserving fish, and clearly states that pickling, which takes place at the end of the sushi-making process, is a means of preserving.

41. **Choice A is correct.** The second paragraph discusses the ways in which sushi has become popular in the U.S. However, it does not mention that it has become more popular than the hamburger.

42. **Choice A is correct.** Something that is a "delicacy" can be described as something that is "choice and expensive."

43. **Choice A is correct.** Because the question refers only to the last paragraph, any opinions that Leonardo's teachers may have elsewhere in the text do not apply. It is true that Leonardo did not get along with the other students (choice J), but nowhere does it say that his teachers had any opinion on this. This is a basic inference question in that the last paragraph states that Leonardo's teachers dreaded his questions because they were sometimes "more than they could answer." From this statement, you can infer that they were afraid they would not have the knowledge to answer his questions and therefore afraid he might ask questions they could not answer.

44. **Choice D is correct.** The text mentions many people as having something to do with raising Leonardo, but line 19 states "It was the old grandmother, Mona Lena, who brought Leonardo up . . ."

45. **Choice A is correct.** When Leonardo was punished for skipping school (lines 62–63), his father locked him in the cupboard, and instead of protesting, he soon found himself lost in his own thoughts. This is how the reader knows that he did not mind being alone, therefore statement I is true. Lines 40-43 show that Leonardo was fascinated by birds and the "secret power in their wings," which makes statement II correct. Lines 24–26 describe Leonardo as not enjoying the company of other boys, from which one can reasonable infer he was not popular, which makes statement III incorrect.

46. **Choice C is correct.** The only date mentioned specifically in the passage is 1492, which was the year of Leonardo's birth. Lines 23–24 state he was seven years old when he was sent to school, which would make the year 1459.

47. **Choice A is correct.** This question asks you to distill a lot of information about Leonardo as a boy and find the one fact that is incorrect. In lines 28–29, it says that Leonardo found Latin grammar "a terrible task," which makes choice A correct.

48. **Choice A is correct.** The lines referred to in the question describe an aspect of Leonardo's personality, but the question asks you to sum up exactly what that aspect is. The line says he "loved the flowers," but he still pulled off their petals because he wanted to understand "how each was joined." Therefore, his desire to learn how things worked was stronger than his affection for nature.

ANSWER EXPLANATIONS FOR PRACTICE TEST 3

WRITING ASSIGNMENT

Life in New York is one of extremes. There is extreme wealth and extreme poverty. There are shiny skyscrapers and buildings that are falling apart. There are busy streets and streets that are almost always empty. Living in New York City means experiencing these opposites. If you were to walk through different parts of Manhattan, you would see many different features, especially if you walked through East Harlem and Wall Street. Although these two places are very different, there is one similarity: in both places, you will find art.

East Harlem is home to many people. However, walking down the streets of East Harlem can make anyone feel melancholy. There are very old buildings and many lonely streets. There are buildings with crumbling facades and many roads with potholes. In many places, there is gang-related graffiti. It is a place where some people would feel uncomfortable to walk in during the day, and scared to walk through at night.

Meanwhile, Wall Street is mainly full of rich and well-dressed people. The buildings are clean, and the people seem focused and busy. You will also see fancy restaurants and you are unlikely to find any graffiti scrawled on the walls.

What many people may not realize is that art can be found in both East Harlem and Wall Street. In East Harlem, there are many street art murals made by local residents. They are big, beautiful and show how happy people are to live there. On 106th Street and Park Avenue, one of these amazing murals can be found at a school's playground. On Wall Street, there is some street art, but the most interesting art is the Charging Bull. It sits right in the middle of everything, and attracts a lot of different people eager to see it and take pictures with it.

There are many differences in both East Harlem and on Wall Street. Although the two places are very different, the art in both locations makes the people who live and work there happy. While some people might consider East Harlem and Wall Street opposites, in truth they are alike. Both are full of life and home to interesting and unique types of art.

ANSWER EXPLANATIONS FOR PRACTICE TEST 3
MATHEMATICS

49. Choice (B) is correct. We have

$$3.2857$$
$$+\ \ 15.9AB9$$
$$19.2636$$

Since 7 + 9 = 16 we carry the 1 and add it to the tens place where we get 1 + 5 + B = 6 + B and this must be equal to 13 (since the digit right below in the outcome is 3). Thus 6 + B = 13 which gives us B = 7. Now, again we need to carry the 1 from 13 and add it to hundredths place where we get 1 + 8 + A = 9 + A and that must be equal to 16 (since the digit right below in the outcome is 6). Thus 9 + A = 16 which gives us A = 7. Thus A − B = 0.

50. Choice (A) is correct. The distance between two numbers that lie on the number line is given by the absolute value of their difference, thus |4.2| - (1.68)| = |4.2 + 1.68| = |5.88. Now if we multiply this number by 0.24 we get 1.4112.

Note: Another way to think about it is to recognize that the distance is close to 6 but smaller, and since 0.24 is about 1/4 we understand that we are looking for a number which will probably be close to and less than 6/4 = 1.5

51. Choice (E) is correct. We have $\frac{3}{5} \div \left(\frac{3}{2}\right)^2 \div \frac{1}{4} = \frac{3}{5} \div \frac{9}{4} \div \frac{1}{4}$

Now as there are two divisions in row and there is no parentheses to indicate the order, it is very critical to do the divisions as they are encountered from left to right:

$$\frac{3}{5} \div \frac{9}{4} \div \frac{1}{4} = \frac{3}{5} \cdot \frac{4}{9} \div \frac{1}{4} = \frac{4}{15} \div \frac{1}{4} = \frac{4}{15} \cdot 4 = \frac{16}{15}$$

52. Choice (C) is correct. We have $\frac{2}{5} \div \frac{6}{25} \cdot \frac{4}{9} = \frac{2}{5} \cdot \frac{25}{6} \cdot \frac{4}{9} = 2 \cdot \frac{5}{3} \cdot \frac{2}{9} = \frac{20}{27}$

53. Choice (B) is correct. We have $\dfrac{\frac{11}{3} \div \frac{1}{4}}{\frac{5}{6} - \frac{7}{3} + 1} = \dfrac{\frac{11}{3} \cdot 4}{\frac{5}{6} - \frac{7}{3} + 1} = \dfrac{\frac{44}{3}}{\frac{5-14+6}{6}} = \dfrac{\frac{44}{3}}{-\frac{1}{2}} = -\frac{88}{3}$

54. Choice (D) is correct. The given pattern 13579111315...., represents all the odd natural numbers in ascending order. We are looking to spot the first 8 that we meet as we go through this sequence that is preceded by 1. The smallest natural number having this property is 18 but it is even, thus not included in the list. Then, one might be tempted to think that the earliest 8 we're looking for is the middle digit of number 181 as no 2-digit natural number (apart from the even 18) fulfills the prerequisite and the first 3-digit number that it does is 181. However if we think a bit deeper on this sequence of digits we'll realize that the digit 8 of number 83 is preceded by the digit 1 of 81. So the 8 that we are looking for is the first digit of number 83 and all we have to do is to spot its position in the above pattern. We observe that for the 2-digit odd numbers, the position of their last digit is always 4 less than the number itself. This is explained by the following: the 1-digit number 9 is the 5th digit in the pattern, so the difference of the odd number and its rank is 4. After number 9, the odds continue to increase by 2 but now they contribute also 2 digits in the pattern, which means that as each 2-digit odd increases by 2, the rank of its last digit also increases by . Thus the difference of the odd number and the rank of its last digit must be stable 4 and this

stays true for all 2-digit odds. Therefore we can find the position of the last digit of number 83 which is 83-4= 79 and by subtracting 1 we finally have the position of 8 (78th)

55. Choice (B) is correct. From 6pm to 7.30pm Sarah has to pay $6. For the remaining time till 11pm (3.5 hours) she will pay 7 x $1.5 = $10.5. Total $6 + $10.5 = $16.5

56. Choice (B) is correct. Since we know that the average score of the first four math test for John was 79%, we also know that their sum is given by 79% + 79% +79% +79% = 316% . With the same logic, since the average of the two last tests is 85%, their sum will equal to 85% + 85% = 170%. The sum of the first four tests along with the sum of the two last tests give the sum of all six tests so 316% + 170% = 486% and thus the average of all six tests is 416% / 6 = 81%

57. Choice (A) is correct. We know that each day Peter is going to get from his account $10 and Julia will add $20. This means that each day their balances will be $30 closer to each other. The initial separation of their accounts is given by $3250 - $1730 = $1530. Thus, if we divide $1530 by $30, we find our answer: 51.

58. Choice (C) is correct. If we line up the 5 children in ascending order we will have _ < _ < S < _ < _ as we know that Suzan gets the middle position. We also know that Greg stands next to her either on the left or on the right. If Greg is older than Suzan then we'll have _ < _ < S < G < and we know that Mat is younger than Greg, which means he has to be in either the first or second position. In addition, Tim is younger than Annie which means that he also needs to be in one of the first two positions or else he would be placed in the fifth position as the oldest one which contradicts the fact that he is younger than Annie. Therefore, Annie should be in the fifth position. If you make Greg younger than Suzan, then since Mat is younger than Greg, he'll take the first position. Additionally Tim is younger than Annie so he has to take the fourth position, leaving the fifth once again for Annie.

59. Choice (A) is correct. We can see from the figure that EO is the radius of the circle, so EO = 5. We can also see that GF is the radius of the semicircle, so GF = 4. GO represents the difference between the two radii, or 1.

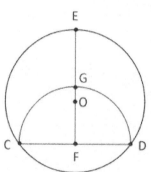

60. Choice (E) is correct. From the sequence 1, 4, 7, 10, 13, 16, 19,… we understand that each natural number is produced by adding three to the previous one. For example if we call the fourth number α_4 we have $\alpha_4 = \alpha_3 + 3$. But it is also true that $\alpha_3 = \alpha_2 + 3$ as well as $\alpha_2 = \alpha_1 + 3$ so the fourth number gets to be $\alpha_4 = \alpha_3 + 3 = (\alpha_2 + 3) + 3 = (\alpha_1 + 3) + 3) + 3 = \alpha_1 + (4-1) \times 3$
And in this way it seems that we came up with a general formula that calculates the th number as $\alpha_n = \alpha_1 + (n-1) \times 3$ and by substituting α_1 and distributing we get $\alpha_n = 3n - 2$. Now if we plug in the number 34 for n we get $\alpha_{34} = 3 \times 34 - 2 = 100$. In order to find the 49th odd natural number we double the number 49 and subtract 1 thus $2 \times 49 - 1 = 97$. (It's easy to see the pattern by taking small odds like 5 which is the 3d odd, 11 which is the 6th odd etc. The formula $\alpha_n = 2n - 1$ gives every odd natural number from its order). Finally 97-100=3

Answer Explanations For Practice Test 3

61. Choice (E) is correct. The formula that gives the th even natural number is $2n$. That's an easy to see conclusion if we take the 1st, 2d, 3d etc even natural numbers and find out that they are all written as 2·1, 2·2, 2·3 etc. respectively. Thus the 17th even natural number is 34. Now it's more of a guess and check work. If we try to start with the primes close to 34, after some trials we see that 34 is written as 31 + 3, 29 + 5, 23 + 11 and 17 + 17. Thus the number of ways that 34 can be written as the sum of two different prime numbers is 3

62. Choice (A) is correct. This problem can be approached a couple of different ways. One way is to think that each person can shake hands with the 6 - 3 = 3 people sitting on the opposite side of the table. (As each person has already shaken hands with the two persons sitting next to it exactly once, the two neighbors and of course itself are excluded). Since there are 6 people on the table, each one of them will initiate 3 handshakes with the three people sitting on the other side of the table and thus the total handshakes will be 6·3 = 18. However this number double counts each handshake as it is counted once when initiated by the one person and it is counted again when initiated by the other person. This means that we need to divide by 2 to find the actual number of unique handshakes, so 18÷2 = 9. This rational applies also when we want to calculate the diagonals of a polygon. We can imagine the six people being on the six vertices of the hexagon, the sides of the hexagon indicate that the handshakes between the neighboring people have been made once and we need to find the remaining handshakes that are represented by the diagonals of the hexagon. Another way to think about it is that the first person who starts to shake hands has three options. The person next to the first has also three options as it has not shaken hands in the first three attempts. The next person has two choices as it has shaken hands with the first. Finally the next person has only one choice as it has shaken hands with the first and the second. The remaining two people will not shake hands as they have already shaken hands with the three on the opposite side when the handshakes were initiated by them. Therefore 3+3+2+1 = 9

63. Choice (E) is correct. The shaded area is comprised of three pieces, a rectangle, a parallelogram and a right triangle. The rectangle's area is 3·2 = 6 (length 3 units, width 2 units). The area of the parallelogram is 3·2 = 6 (length units, height units). The area of the right triangle is $\frac{3 \cdot 3}{2} = 4.5$ (base 3 units, height 3 units). Thus the total area will be 6 + 6 + 4.5 = 16.5 squared units.

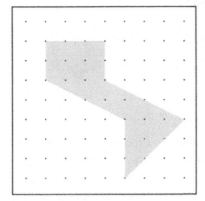

64. Choice (C) is correct. We have a 3-digit number with A first digit which is multiplied with a 2-digit number with also A first digit, and the product has 20 in its first two digits. From this we can suspect what A must be. A cannot be 5 or more because the product 555 with 5B (whatever B is) would exceed 25,000. A cannot also be 3 or less because 333 times 3B (whatever B is) cannot even get close to 20,000 (even if B is 9 we have approximately 40 times 333 which is something around 13,000). Thus A must be 4. Then B must be 2 or 7 as these are the only digits that when

multiplied by 4 give a number ending with 8 as the last digit of the outcome is. With a few tries we see that B must be 7.
Or, simple trial-and-error shows that A must be 4, since a 3-digit number beginning with 4 times a 2-digit number beginning with 4 is the only option for producing the product of 20,868.

65. Choice (B) is correct. The interest of the first year was $500 · 4% = $20 and the balance increased to $520. Thus the interest for the second year was $520 · 4% = $20.8 and the balance increased to $540.8. Therefore, the interest for the third year was $540.8 · 4% = $21.632. Now, if we add the 3 interest amounts we will find the total interest paid into the account.
$20 + $20.8 + $21.632 = $62.432 and by getting the fraction 62.432/500 we see that the total interest paid into the account is approximately 12.5% of the initial deposit.

66. Choice (D) is correct. First of all we can see that there are 3 steps that we need to go through to order a pizza: a) crust selection, b) size selection and c) toppings selection.
This now becomes a traditional "combinations" problem. We are making 3 choices, so we multiply the number of options within each choice: 3 x 3 x 4 = 36.

67. Choice (B) is correct. If we assume that the initial price of the piano when it was bought by John was $100, then we know that John sold it to Peter for 25% more, thus $100 + $100 · 25% = $125. Now we know that Peter sold this piano to Emma for 13% less than he had paid to John, so $125 + $125 · 13% = $108.75. Thus amount that Emma paid for the piano as a percent of the original price is 108.75/100 ≅ 109%

68. Choice (C) is correct. We know that if in the first case, where Mary had more money, she would buy 120 candies, while in the second case, where Mary had less money she would buy 85 candies. So there are 120 – 85 = 35 candies that can be bought with the $3.20 more and the $2.40 less than the money she actually has. This means that $3.20 + $2.40 = $5.60 buys 35 candies and thus the price per candy must be $5.60 / 35 = $0.16 or 16¢

69. Choice (D) is correct. If we mark each distinct area with letters as shown below, we'll be helped in figuring out all -sided figures in this diagram. The following areas or combinations of them generate one 4-sided figure each:
A&B , B , B&C&D , B&C , C&D , C , F&D&E , F&D , F&G , F&G&C&D , F&G&C&D&E

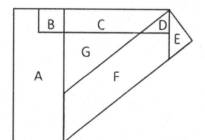

70. Choice (D) is correct. We know that the shape of both pools is a rectangular prism. From the formula $V = l \cdot w \cdot h$ that gives the volume of a rectangular prism, we calculate the volume of the big pool when the height of the water is 1.8 meters, thus 15·7·1.8 = 189 cubic meters. Since we want the volume of the kid's pool to be 10% of the volume of the big pool, we can calculate the volume of the kid's pool as 10%·189 = 18.9 cubic meters. And applying the above formula on kid's pool we get 6·5·h = 18.9, therefore 30·h = 18.9 and thus height of the water in the kid's pool will be h = 30/18.9 = 0.63 meters

71. Choice (D) is correct. We know that A and B photocopy machines combined can print 2,070 pages in half an hour or 30 minutes. This means that the two machines combined can print 2,070 / 30 = 69 pages per minute. We also know that machine A is twice as fast as machine B. This means that if the 69 pages were divided to 3 equal parts, 2 parts would have been produced by A and 1 part by B. Thus machine B produces 69 / 3 = 23 pages per minute and machine A produces

Answer Explanations For Practice Test 3

2·23 = 46 pages per minute. Now we know that both machines worked together for 10 minutes before a third one joins them. Therefore machines A and B combined produced 10·69 = 690 pages during that 10 minutes. The remaining work to be done at that point of time was 2,070 − 690 = 1380 pages and a third machine C as fast as A (with 46 pages per minute capacity) enters the production process. Now the three machines combined can print 23 + 46 + 46 = 115 pages per minute. Thus the 1,380 remaining pages can be printed in 1,380 / 115 = 12 minutes. So the total time spent in printing was 10 + 12 = 22 minutes, 8 minutes earlier than half an hour

72. Choice (D) is correct. No matter the shape of the AB line, as long as there are no diagonal moves and all the horizontal pieces add to 5 and the vertical pieces add to 3, both George and Harry walked 5 + 3 = 8 hundred meters each in their route from A to B. Similarly, George walked 3 + 5 = 8 hundred meters from B to C and Harry walked 5 + 5 = 10 hundred meters going from B to D. Therefore, total distance covered by both:
(5 + 3 + 3 + 5) + (5 + 3 + 5 + 5) = 34 hundred meters thus 3,400 meters

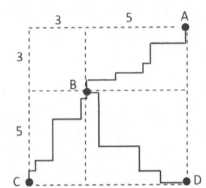

73. Choice (C) is correct. Any number that is divisible by 6 is at the same time divisible by 2 and 3 because these two numbers divide 6. So, BC must be even and divisible by 3, or BC must be even and the sum of its digits must be divisible by 3. BC can be formed by 2, 5, 6 and 7 each used once. To be even, its last digit must be either 2 or 6. The combinations for BC are 56, 76, 26, 62, 52 and 72. Only the last one is divisible by 3 because 7 + 2 = 9. Thus BC = 72. Now the options for A are either 5 or 6 but only 6 makes the sum of the digits divisible by 3 (6 + 7 + 2 = 15). Therefore ABC = 672

74. Choice (A) is correct. If we represent with x the number of people in the town that voted for 2 candidates, then we know that these people gave totally $2 \cdot x$ votes. We also know that same number of people (the other half, thus x again) voted for 3 candidates. So, these people gave $3 \cdot x$ votes. Therefore the total votes that were given by all people in the small town were $2 \cdot x + 3 \cdot x = 5 \cdot x$. But we know that the total votes that were counted for candidates A, B, C and D were 243 + 191 + 186 + 160 = 780. So, 780 must be equal to $5 \cdot x$ and thus x = 780 / 5 = 156. From this we get the total voters $x + x = 156 + 156 = 312$

75. Choice (B) is correct. The baker will need to make something like the grid depicted in the second figure which is comprised by 2 horizontal pieces and 4 vertical pieces. Each horizontal piece has length equal to the box's length, while each vertical piece has length equal to the width of the box. The length of the box is equal to the sum of the diameters of the 5 muffins that are placed horizontally and the width of the box equals the sum of the diameters of the 3 muffins placed vertically. Thus, length = 5·2 = 10 and width = 3·2 = 6 (where the diameter of a muffin is 2 times its radius, so 2·1 = 2). Therefore the total pieces that the baker will need to make the below grid is 2·10 + 4·6 = 44 inches

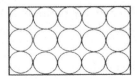
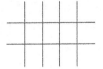

76. Choice (B) is correct. Since the slowest train is traveling with 90 miles per hour, this means that in 1 minute it travels 90/60 = 1.5 miles. So, in 25 minutes it will cover 25·1.5 = 37.5 miles of the total 87.5 that the two trains are apart. And from this it is implied that during these 25 minutes the fastest train will cover the remaining 50 miles, so its speed will be 50/25 = 2 miles per minute. Which leads us to a speed of 2·60 = 120 miles per hour

77. Choice (E) is correct. What we firstly need to think here is that this cube is made of 6 stacked layers of small 1 x 1 x 1 cubes (unit cubes). The bottom layer is shown in the below figure on the right. As we see this layer, as well as any other, is comprised of 6·6 = 36 unit cubes, from which the invisible ones could be those shaded in grey which are 4·4 = 16. Now, starting from the ground and moving up in each layer we will count 5 layers from which the shaded area could be missing. The 6th layer on the top of the cube has all its unit cubes because it is visible to us and we see them. Therefore the biggest number of unit cubes that could be missing is 16·5 = 80

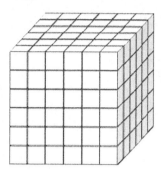

78. Choice (C) is correct. We write down the 2-digit number as AB. Then we know that A represents the tens and B the units which means that the AB can be written as A·10 + B·1. Now if we reverse the digits of this number we get the number BA which also can be written as B·10+A·1. We know that BA is greater than AB (because AB increases when its digits reverse) and we also know that the difference of the two numbers is 36, thus 36 = BA – AB or 36 = B·10 + A·1 – (A·10 + B·1) or 36 = 10B + A – 10A – B or 36 = 9B – 9A or 36 = 9(B – A) and finally B – A = 36/9 = 4. And since we want to find the first digit of AB minus its second digit we get A – B = – 4

79. Choice (D) is correct. We know that of the number of bacteria in a day, the 3/4 are new bacteria. This means that the remaining 1/4 must be coming from the previous day. And since the total number of bacteria is represented by 4/4, the increase in one day is $\frac{4}{4} \div \frac{1}{4} = 1 \cdot \frac{4}{1} = 4$ times. Now if a the number increases 4 times in one day and the new number increases again 4 times in the next day, the total increase will be 4·4 = 16 (consider number 1 which increases 4 times in one day and becomes 4·1=4 and then the new number 4 increases again 4 times and becomes 4·4 = 16)

80. Choice (C) is correct. We have 10 numbers from 1 to 10, so all multiples of 6 from 1·6 = 6 up to 10·6 = 60 are 10.
66 is also a multiple of 6 but we do not include it as we want numbers smaller than 66.
From the above 10 multiples of 6 we exclude the 1·6 = 6 as we are interested in two-digit numbers. So there are 9 two-digit multiples of 6 which are less than 66. With the same logic there are 13 multiples of 5 between 1 and 50. We exclude 1·5 = 5 because is a single-digit number so we have 12 multiples of 5 less than 66.
So far we have 9 multiples of 6 plus 12 multiples of 5, total 21 numbers. Now we need to identify the common multiples of both 6 and 5 and subtract them once because we have counted them twice. These are the least common multiple of 5 and 6 and any multiple of it which is less than 66. The least common multiple is 5·6 = 30 so the numbers we need to exclude are 30 and 2·30 = 60. So total number is 21 – 2 = 19.

Answer Explanations For Practice Test 3

81. Choice (C) is correct. The least amount Sandy could have is when she has 2 pennies and 1 nickel which means 2·1 + 1·5 = 7 cents. The next amount she could have is when she has 3 pennies and 2 nickels which means that the initial amount of 7 cents would increase by 1 penny and 1 nickel, thus 6 cents. So all possible amounts would be the sum of 7 and a multiple of 6. Therefore, from the given choices we need to subtract 7 and check if they are multiples of 6. The only one who is not a multiple of 6 when 7 is subtracted is 59 because 59 − 7 = 52 which is not divisible by 6. All the remaining choices are possible amounts

82. Choice (E) is correct. Let's interpret each of the i) ii) and iii).
    i) When a number leaves a remainder 2 when divided by 4, it means that it is composed by a multiple of 4 plus 2. For instance, 4 + 2 = 6, 2(4) + 2 = 10, etc. These numbers will all be even.
    ii) When a number leaves remainder 3 when divided by 5, it means that it must be a multiple of 5 plus 3. All multiples of 5 have as a last digit 0 or 5, so the number will end in 3 or 8. And since from i) we know that it is even, we conclude that the number must end to 8.
    iii) When a number leaves a remainder of 1 when divided by 3, it means that it can be written as a multiple of 3 plus 1. This means that the previous number is a multiple of 3, so the sum of its digits is divisible by 3. Thus the sum of the digits of our number is a multiple of 3 plus 1. Now we first write down all 2-digit numbers that are even and end to eight: 18, 28, 38, 48, 58, 68, 78, 88, 98. Then we are looking for the numbers that when we subtract 1 from the sum of their digits we get a number that is divisible by 3. The only numbers that do this are 28, 58 and 88. Finally, we cross off the numbers that are divisible by 4, which are 28 and 88, and that leaves 58 as the answer.

83. Choice (B) is correct. In the bottom right quarter of the circle we have a segment that has 3 inches length and a vertical segment with 4 inches length. By dividing the 4-inch segment into 4 1-inch segments we can cut 4 3-inch by 1-inch rectangles. And because there are 4 quarters in the circle we can totally have 4·4 = 16 3-inch by 1-inch as shown in the figure on the left. Now on the right side of the circle we can draw a similar to the 6-inch segment which now will be vertical and will be split into two equal 3-inch parts by the horizontal diameter of the circle. Its distance from the center of the circle will similarly be 4 inches from which the 3 inches have already been cut in the previous phase. Thus two more 3-inch by 1-inch rectangles are created with their length being ver-tical this time (see figure on the right). Another 2 similar rectangles will be created in the left side of the circle thus total 3-inch by 1-inch rectangles: 16 + 2 + 2 = 20

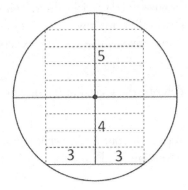 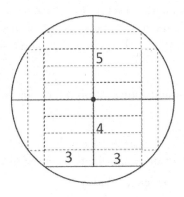

ESSAY PROMPTS

Writing Assignment #1

Every borough in New York City has distinctions that make it stand out from the other boroughs. Every borough has its own character and unique flavor.

Your neighborhood within your borough stands out from other neighborhoods, too. What sights, sounds and smells make up your neighborhood? Who are the people in your neighborhood?

Take a moment to picture who they are, what family members and friends they have, and what makes them unique. Think about what they say, how they dress and the stories they tell.

Write an essay or tell a story that shows what your neighborhood is like. Include descriptions of the physical surroundings and create a picture of the people who live there by focusing on one or two neighbors and explaining what they are like.

- Write the real names of streets and neighborhood or borough landmarks,
- Include sensory details so that your reader might easily identify the unique neighborhood where you live.
- Change the real names of people if you would like, and
- Add dialogue where it might be appropriate.

Writing Assignment #2

Many people like to go on adventures where they see and do new things that most other people don't get to do. They want to experience the extraordinary, like riding on an elephant or white water rafting across a swirling river. For them, exotic and unusual moments are exciting.

You may be one of those people.

Extraordinary moments, however, don't have to be exotic. They just have to be special to you. Think about some of the simple things in your life that have been very special to you. Perhaps it was a sunset of incredible color, a small gift, or a chance for peace and quiet in a space all your own. These, too, are extraordinary moments.

Which special moment comes to mind for you? How would you describe the special moment you experienced?

Your task is to write an essay or a story. In the writing, you will describe for your reader what you saw and what you felt during an extraordinary moment in your life. Include special details, such as

- What you experienced with your senses
- What feelings you had and still have about the moment, and
- Why this extraordinary moment was so special.

Essay Prompts

Writing Assignment #3

The kitchen is often called the heart of a home. Sooner or later, it's the one place everyone goes. It's where you find food, water, conversation, and even comfort.

Your kitchen may be the space for more than food preparation. It's also where people gather, homework gets done and conversations are held. Every kitchen has its own smells and sounds.

What is the kitchen of your home like? Close your eyes for a moment and imagine you are there, in your kitchen at home. What do you see? What smells comes from the kitchen? Are they pleasant or irritating smells? What noises do you hear?

Your kitchen may be a busy and happy place where many people gather, or it may be a practical space for light snacks and quick meals. There is no one kind of kitchen that is better than another.

Write a descriptive essay that creates a picture of your kitchen. Include

- The physical description of the kitchen,
- As many sensory images as you can, and
- Your personal assessment of your kitchen; what do you like or dislike about it?

Writing Assignment #4

School is required for every student. Fortunately, there are many different types of schools available to students in New York City. You could attend a Public School, a charter school, a private or parochial school, or you could even be homeschooled.

At some point in your school career, the location of your schooling will change. Finding out that you are going to a new school can cause anxiety, but it can also be fun. Although schools all have similarities to each other, some schools are very different from each other.

For example, attending a traditional P.S. (public school) in New York City may be different than attending one of the charter schools or private schools in the city. Even getting to the new school every day may be a different experience for you.

What would worry you or please you about attending a new school?

Write an essay that explains your concerns or your excitement about moving to a new school. Be sure to include

- What your current school is like,
- What you imagine the new school to be like, and
- Why you would be worried or happy about going to a new school.

Writing Assignment #5

People who live outside New York City may feel like they know a thing or two about the five boroughs that make up the Big Apple. In fact, they may have some stereotypes about Brooklyn, the Bronx, Queens, Staten Island and Manhattan. A stereotype categorizes people or places by putting them all together in one group, even though not every person or place fits the stereotype.

Your task is to identify and eliminate a common stereotype about your borough. For example, is the Bronx a better place to grow up in than Brooklyn? Does everyone who lives in Brooklyn really want to move to Manhattan? Do all of the people who live in Manhattan have a doorman and ride in taxis everywhere they go?

Think about a common stereotype of the borough where you live. What is that stereotype? How true is it?

For this assignment, you will bust the stereotype of your borough by writing an essay in which you clearly identify a stereotype about your borough and show why it is not true.

- Explain what the stereotype is,
- Tell why the stereotype is not true, and
- Give examples that show this stereotypes is not valid.

Writing Assignment #6

New York City has many layers: different neighborhoods coexisting; above ground/underground; newcomers/oldcomers; work/home.

Your task is to write about different layers of New York that you have passed through or continuously pass through. You could choose to write about a bus journey through different neighborhoods, your trip to a fancy overpriced boutique versus the bargain-priced consignment store, or the transition from being with friends at school to your family life at home.

In this essay, you will:

- Compare and contrast two 'layers' that are generally from the same category or general type of thing or idea;
- Provide details and elaboration that explain how you move through "layers" in your life;
- Explain the differences and similarities in the layers;
- Describe how your journey through the layers helps you understand the diversity of places and people in New York City.

Writing Assignment #7

Describe a "first time" experience you had in New York City and what it revealed to you about yourself and the city. For example, you could describe your first subway ride, first meal at a food truck, first day at a new school.

Your task is to describe an experience that allows the reader to experience a small corner of our city. Your essay should use sensory detail (the five senses: sight, sound, smell, touch, and taste) to describe this experience and to reveal what it means to you.

Made in United States
North Haven, CT
17 January 2025

64580275R00063